Out and Around in Lockdown

Out and Around in Lockdown

A Record

March 2020–August 2021

**A memoir for a time like no other by
Wendy Funnell**

Matador
Unit E2 Airfield Business Park,
Harrison Road, Market Harborough,
Leicestershire. LE16 7UL
Tel: 0116 2792299
Email: books@troubador.co.uk
Web: www.troubador.co.uk/matador
Twitter: @matadorbooks

ISBN 978 1803132 006

British Library Cataloguing in Publication Data.
A catalogue record for this book is available from the British Library.

Printed and bound in the UK by TJ Books LTD, Padstow, Cornwall
Typeset in 11pt Adobe Caslon Pro by Troubador Publishing Ltd, Leicester, UK

Matador is an imprint of Troubador Publishing Ltd

About the Book

When Covid and lockdown came upon us in the spring of 2020 no-one could know how it was going to work out for them individually. My expectation was that in general we would win through but how long that would take, and how it would be to live through this unique period were all quite unclear. So firstly, I would like to thank family, friends and the community of Worthing, West Sussex for supporting me through Covid in a general way; and to this the book is testament.

The book came about because, as a long-term diarist, I decided to keep a record in the form of blogs written, in an 'as it happens' manner, of what it was like to be in lockdown, doing it my way, and adjusting to the changes to the rules. My thanks also go, therefore to those who enjoyed the original blogs, who continue to read the occasional blog I still contribute on **https://steppingoutandlookingaboutincovidtimes.wordpress.com** and who have also encouraged me to seek publication in book form, as follows. So, the book consists of the blogs largely as written but set in the added context of the relevant Lockdown laws and the rise and fall of Covid numbers.

Contents

June – Hold-Up!

July – We Think It's All Over?

Postscript

The Shock of Lockdown

People must stay home, and preferably work from home. They should leave only if essential such as for shopping, or medical care. People may exercise, but one household alone and once a day only. Social distancing (two metres apart) has to be maintained.

Non-essential high street businesses must close, including personal care.

Hospitality venues must close, also other premises such as libraries, outdoor gyms and places of worship.[1]

---

1   For source details of this and similar headings, please see PS 1.

1. Introduction: What's Going On?

25 March 2020[2]

How are we to know the streets are empty in lockdown, the roads silent? What does 'lockdown' mean? What is life going to be like in lockdown? Someone needs to go outside just to say there is nobody outside! These are historic times and need to be recorded. And so, I'm writing blogs, as and when, for several reasons.

Because of lockdown, we are on our own in many ways, not just in a general way from friends and family but in many small ways also. We are having to make decisions on the spot about where and how we move about or having to think about how we do what we have been doing for years without much thought. These blogs are to show that we all have these problems and maybe also to show some answers.

Thereby, also, I hope that those who cannot get out can also read these and understand a little of what's happening 'out there' and so, when the time comes and they can rejoin the world, it will not seem too alien from them. There's nothing so bizarre as normal life when you're not living it. And finally,

---

2   The date is when the blog was posted, not necessarily when it was written nor of the event(s) described in it.

in due course, we shall be back to normal, whatever that is, and we shall forget how we lived life in Covid times. Or we shall remember these strange times as a dream, hopefully not a nightmare, and want to know: did it really happen?

Lockdown has put us into particular categories, and I have decided that, while I must admit myself into the 'old' category, I do not admit to being 'elderly' and, thankfully, not 'vulnerable'. I take no credit for this. It's just my good fortune. And I will continue to do my own shopping and not take advantage of any supermarket's offer of priority. And take advantage of the 'out for exercise' dispensation. Long years ago, when my father died suddenly, my mother was advised to go out for a walk, or at least out, every day. It stood her in good stead, and I think it will me too.

I have also a history of engaging with the street scene, as off and on over the years I have done a fair bit of market research interviewing. It's a funny thing to go stand on some street corner in a not-familiar town to ask people questions about whatever they used, or did, and possibly why, then to get the brush-off from some or to try to stop the flow from others. But I enjoyed it.

Also, until about four years ago I delivered, every week, the free paper in my local Durrington area of Worthing. Being paid to walk seemed a good idea! I became accustomed to putting aside one morning for that and, even better, the family also became used to that and let me be in peace that day. I was mostly lucky with the weather. For the five years I delivered a Friday paper it scarcely ever rained on Friday. That paper ceased and I transferred to a Wednesday paper.

My luck with the weather did not continue but I became fairly expert in judging whether I could get the round finished before rain and worse struck, or at least how far round the course. I trust that judgement will stay with me. It is only too easy to look out the window and see a bit of rain, hear the wind blowing a bit and think, 'I can't go out there'. Whereas, when a worker, you would put on a thicker coat, go out the front door from habit and only half-way to work think, 'the weather's terrible!'

However, the internet and Google made free papers obsolete and for the second time I was paid redundancy money. The first redundancy money contributed to a splendid holiday travelling east across Russia to Vladivostok, and the second to a coach tour of the Outer Hebrides. But I resolved to keep the habit and continued out walking the local area every Wednesday.

It is intentionally more or less the same route every week. It means I do not have to think too hard about where to go; indeed, there is something reassuring in the fact that I know where I'm going. I can get into my stride quickly and just carry on. There is enough variety and contrast in the housing styles to take an interest. Durrington is a part of Worthing where, until recently, only a few houses at a time were put up by a local small builder. Worthing is, in a way, a collection of small old villages such as Durrington joined together.

I am grateful now that I have maintained the Wednesday walk habit and intend to use that for the exercise break which we are now allowed to take. However, I am troubled by how long our exercise break is meant to be. All day? Is there a time specified? I suspect that by exercise they mean about one hour. So, I am breaking up my standard route into that kind of time and distance.

For my first outing, I was helped on my way by blue sky and warm sunshine. I walked northward through the latest housing development. It is still growing there but I was somewhat surprised to see a man driving a loader truck around and he was as surprised to see me walking there.

We were both slightly dubious about the legality of the other's actions. Then through the last remaining field of the area to an old coaching inn on the A27 and circuitously homeward. I met about half a dozen dogwalkers, all pleased to say 'Good morning' from a safe distance and move out the way; otherwise, the peace and quiet of suburbia. Lovely smell of new-mown grass and birdsong everywhere; a roofer trying to finish the job; a homeowner looking at his half-finished new drive then down the empty road for any sign of his contractor coming his way.

Home again after one and a half hours – hope that's OK. Over my second breakfast I reflected that I had made my point about going out. The outside is still there, and I had maintained my right to go there. But I had also missed the point. My familiarity with the area made me blind to the unfamiliar. I had been deaf to the silence, unmoved by the stillness; the unreality of it all had gone unseen. Life in lockdown is not going to be exciting (I hope) but what it is like to be in lockdown is going to be interesting, in its own strange way.

While we must stay local, it will be the small details that become important. That is the story of everyone's life at present as we learn to negotiate the new world of the unfamiliar familiar. The stories may take place in my local area, but they are the stories of everyone in their local area.

I had just enough energy left to join my online Silver Swans[3] ballet group! It's just like walking, isn't it? Especially the way I do it.

Galumph to the right, galumph to the left.
Oh, sorry. Wrong way round!

3   https://www.royalacademyofdance.org/dance-with-us/silver-swans/

2. Where Is Everyone?

26 March 2020

I started to record in my diary the cumulative numbers of cases of Covid-19 in UK as given by the BBC, but am giving here the daily number of cases by date reported, from the Government Covid Dashboard.[4]
No. of UK cases: 2,129

Quite amazed that, in what would be the rush hour in normal times, I was able to cross the A259 by the Centenary House roundabout without having to use the zebra crossing and the lights. But it was even more peaceful to take the pink public access path through Westlake Gardens and watch the small fountain in the lake ceaselessly at work. The wind was keen, so I was quite glad to turn south and, by degrees, make my way through Tarring churchyard, filled with white and pink blossoming trees. It was probably too early for the children's playground to be in use, though older children were larking about on the netball court, while mum sat by. Or is the children's playground out of bounds too, even to children?

---

[4] Source for this and similar information throughout the book: https://coronavirusdata.gov.uk/details; public sector information licensed under Open Government Licence v3.0. (November 2021)

Princess Avenue is also lined by trees, but even more so these days by cars, head to tail down both sides – thousands of pounds' worth of metal standing there, unused. Builders' merchants were delivering pallet after pallet of bricks, sand etc. over the wall to someone's back garden. Will they be allowed to use it and get the job done, whatever it is? Maybe I shall find out in the next few weeks.

I turned along the footpath by the allotments. Tall flats are close by – none have balconies – how difficult to be enclosed in one of those for weeks. Ten cars were in the allotment's car park, but I could spy only two people working on their plots. The footpath is long and narrow, and I wondered what the etiquette was if another walker came the other way. Should we pass back-to-back, or just try not to breathe out at each other? But then, how do you say, 'Good day'? That now seems to be a very necessary part of being out and about.

Back on a main road, the no.10 bus passed on the most circuitous tour of Worthing. In normal times it would have been packed with OAPs taking an early 'free' bus into town. It was totally empty of passengers. The driver had the bus all to himself.

I walked the last few yards home with the wind cold in my face and, as usual, looked up to see High Salvington Windmill on the line of the hills, above and at the back of the town. It had been turned to face the wind, today from the north, so not the usual sight of the white sweeps but of the white door into the black body of the mill, closed. It was as if the mill, too, had turned its back on the world, turned away from its community into its own private life. Home again just in time for a little something.

3. It's Gone Quiet

27 March 2020

No. of UK cases: 2,890

The sky still cloudless blue and warming sunshine diluting the easterly breeze, I set out up the white concrete road of a 1960s (or so) bungalow estate with wide, grassed front gardens, not many flowers, and more lamp posts than trees. Because it is so spacious and open it is also bright and light even on dull dark days. Some roads seem so closed in, so dark with black tarmac pavements, even more so if tall houses mean the sun must rise quite high before any light and warmth fall on the passer-by. Then I stepped through the slot in the big hedge and into a little copse of birdsong and daffodils. It backs onto the playing fields of the primary school, now sadly silent, still and lifeless. In fact, the whole area was! Social distancing was at 200 metres, if as close. Only a black-and-white cat leisurely crossed the road, confident in its survival chances. The net-curtained, vertical-shuttered windows of the houses hid any movement inside. It was not peace and quiet, it was almost frightening.

A little more life in the park, where a hoodied young man (6ft) played goalie as his son (2ft) kicked the ball (1ft) more or less in his direction and young daughter

(3ft) eschewed the male preoccupation with ball games to indulge in the joy of running, around. Indeed, I could people the empty streets with memories of kindness from my paper delivery days. Somehow, in pushing the papers through a letterbox I had drawn blood from the backs of the fingers, and it was flowing remarkably freely. A gardener nearby saw my plight and produced plaster and bandage and tidied me up. Thereafter, I carried plasters and bandage with me! It was in that tradition, I felt, that I saw a car draw up. Mum (I suppose) stayed in the driver's seat while teenager got out, and walked over to Gran, shielding behind the barely opened front door, to pass across a bag of necessities. Family waves and blown kisses followed.

The hamlet of Salvington includes several useful retail outlets and a pub – all shut. And one store open, outside of which a queue had formed, its members the regulation two-metre distance apart. A departing customer had eggs among her shopping – so I was quite tempted to join. Why are eggs so difficult to buy? Have the hens stopped laying? I did not join the queue but posted cards to two friends who are not into modern tech. Another shopper came along wearing a mask! Do not think of a white surgical face mask, but more like a full-blown diver's mask! And through it came a song.

I fell over several years back, in Salvington, not delivering papers just walking, due to an unhappy conjunction of raised paving stone, wrong part of the stride and bad luck. Immediately someone rushed out from their office to pick me up. Fortunately, the only damage was a cut lip to show for it. Since then, I have taken to walking in the road. That way it is easier to see the enemy coming. I had never expected to do that in Salvington Road, with its school, church, shops at both ends and a frequent bus route – and it is a useful link road – nor did I even today, but it was almost possible, so few and far between was the traffic. The question is which side of the road to walk on, as one side can be shady but the other in the sun.

A big car drew up in front of a house. The driver picked up a shopping bag of goodies from the boot and delivered it in a brisk but friendly fashion to a welcoming front door, then drove off. There had been several such bags in the car, so I had no doubt I was witness to an errand of mercy of some kind.

The school, seen from this side, surprisingly *was* open! Some cars were in the car park. The front door was open in a restricted way with a box of pears left beside it. Big happy rainbows had been painted in the windows. Presumably the students are the children of NHS workers and key workers, and so are quick off the mark with this NHS support sign.

I had hoped to do a little shopping, but my usual shop was closed for a delivery. An hour later I returned. It had opened as promised. Will there be eggs? A queue had already formed, one person being allowed in as another left. I was about tenth in line and, as we were all doing our best at social distancing, the queue was round the corner and in the shade. It was progress just to move on and reach the sunny side. And after half an hour I was into the shop. No eggs! But the morning had been enriched by the experience of kindness past and present.

4. The Rainbow

31 March 2020

No. of UK cases: 3,250

What is everyone *doing* behind the blinds? I walked out through the interesting nearby complex of houses and pathways, so designed (it seemed) that one moment I was walking past a front garden, and the next a back garden. No sound from either and no one was outside. So, into Whitebeam Woods, a place of trees and shadows where, after all these years, I am never sure I am on the right path for my intended exit. It's lovely in bluebell time. But beside its dark, still pond someone had abandoned their pink jumpsuit trousers. I hoiked them out of the trees with my stick, then had to carry them until, in the next housing complex, I found someone's bin beside the path with the lid open, so dumped them in!

I was feeling not exactly lost but a bit mislaid among all the houses hereabouts and the maze of twittens,[5] paths and throughways that connect them. Many of these were covered with the twigs, branches and small stuff brought

---

5   *Twitten* – a Sussex word, possibly short for 'betwixt and between'. It refers to the urban equivalent of a footpath, i.e., a narrow alleyway between buildings.

down by Storms Ciara, Dennis and Jorge over the last few weeks. It was relentlessly silent until, from a first floor flat came a loud blast of reggae; not my music, but I was glad to hear anything. I crossed the traffic-free road and located two adjacent footpaths and took not the signed footpath but the tarmac path alongside.

This came to a dead end with piles of brambles and more, but also an opening through which to sidestep into the newish housing estate built there. At its centre is a very attractive little undulating copse, with meandering paths and big boulders to sit or play on. Nobody there! But it's *always* been full of children larking around, and their happy laughter. Then I read the notice. All children's play areas are closed due to the virus; no one should enter. How sad! But in a neighbouring house and garden someone was trying to entertain the family, causing shrieks of laughter and balls banging the wall.

I came out by Northbrook College[6] (closed) and crossed over on the footbridge. A no.9 bus came by on its remarkable route across West Sussex which, fortunately, went close both to my sister's road and mine. It stopped by the college, and someone got out – did it actually have a passenger? No, it was the driver so ahead of schedule that he had time to stop and have a breather before the due moment to move on.

I walked down Goring Street beside the rife[7] that surfaces here. There was quite a flow in it as the water from the various winterbournes of the area had by this time collected up. The May Bridge is not marked on the land though shown on the map. It seems now an access

6   Northbrook College, https://www.gbmc.ac.uk
7   *Rife* – a Sussex word that refers to a flow of water that is larger than a stream but not big enough to be a river.

path for the farmer to get his machinery into the field just before the rife turns to the west and heads for the big Ferring Rife. Dog walkers use it as well.

Looking across the field towards Highdown Hill, I could see a police car sitting in the layby on the south side of the Littlehampton Road. Was he there to demand of drivers their reasons for their journey? However, as there was nobody outside the car, and such cars as there were, were not being stopped, maybe he too was having a breather. I was held up at the level crossing as a train pulled out of Goring Station heading for Southampton – one person per coach, as far as I could see. There's social distancing for you!

I headed home along The Pallant, the paved walkway between houses hereabout. At last, people in the streets! Two red-jacketed postmen and an orange-jacketed water meter reader. But among a group of useful shops, all closed, a convenience store was open. Did they have eggs? I was still on the hunt. Indeed so, and from the back of the shop was brought a tray of eggs. A tray of 30 eggs! For a moment I contemplated buying them. Then common sense took over. How was I going to carry a tray of eggs? I could scarcely put them in my daysac and I was still 20 minutes' walk from home – I was working on an average time of an hour or so, or maybe seven hours a week, or just not bothering too much now about the detail. In any case, it would mean a diet of eggs for days. Reluctantly I declined.

A final walk through 'Little Canada' (the streets and roads have Canadian placenames) and someone *had* been active. A rainbow in crayons on the pavement and with it the slogan 'There is always a rainbow after the storm'.

5. If Not Here, Where?

6 April 2020

No. of UK cases: 4,143

With some alarm, I realised last week that my walking shoes were absolutely shot through; very little rubber was left on the sole, and the heel quite worn down. Assuming clothes and shoe shops are among those classed as non-essential retail, they are now shut. In any case, should any be open, they are down in central Worthing, and that, being beyond my local domain, is now almost the Forbidden City. I realised I would have to look online. Years ago, I had bought a few items of clothing from mail-order catalogues, but, when those colourful, cheerful print productions largely ceased, I had not switched to online. I have bought plenty of things online, but not fashion. In any case, buying shoes is different: you really do need to try them on and walk up and down in the shops to see how well they work for your own feet.

At least I could have a look and from habit started with a general online supplier. Something looked quite hopeful, but then I discovered that regular delivery was up to one month, or special delivery (in a week) carried a heavy charge. I looked at an online shoe shop, found something hopeful and read the reviews which, as usual, said some people liked them, they fitted some people, and others not at all. The colour was pleasing anyway – what a way to buy walking shoes! They were a bit cagey about delivery but were not off-putting, so I paid the money.

A couple of days later, I had an email from the courier saying the shoes were at the local depot. And, later, a second to say they would be delivered that evening between 7 and 9pm. It also gave advice about how to avoid contact with the driver (or should it be vice versa?). Accordingly, I put a stool outside in the porch as a go-between and waited. Nine o'clock came and went and no shoes!

But at 2115 the knock came, and I found the courier to be standing back from the door, taking a photo, seemingly of my packet. He put the pack down on the stool – no signature required. I asked him, maintaining social distance, if I was his last call and he said 'almost' and went off in a surprisingly unhurried way. I was drop 72! Half an hour later, an email came that said my parcel had been delivered and a little map to show just where. Oh good: my house! And about the same time an email from the shoe people to say the shoes would be delivered in the next seven days! They were right about that.

So, what were the shoes like? They fitted quite well lengthwise, happily long enough for me. But I have a problem toe on the left foot – it doesn't seem to want to bend where the shoe does – so I spent the next day walking around the house to see how that would pan out. This at least gave more time than one has in the shop and a slightly more realistic walking situation. It seemed possible. The real problem was the colour.

I had ordered brown, but an odd grey had been delivered. Should I send it back and ask for an exchange, or be thankful for what I had received? Back to the shop website where I found they do not exchange by post, only in the shop. So, I would have to claim a refund, and start again with a reorder. Was this a mistake in the picking? Or was the choice at that very moment these or nothing, so they sent these? I decided to settle for what I had. And walked up to the shops in them, irredeemably to make them mine. They are quite comfortable, but I'm still not taken by the colour.

I waited in the queue separated by the two-metre tape on the pavement (or four paving slabs) and was quite surprised to see two people wearing face masks. And was somewhat amused, when I was allowed in, to see that one of them was at the till with the assistant and not at the self-service checkout, and, more so, that the assistant could not hear what was being said, so the mask had to be removed!

I do now have eggs! On a last journey out in the old shoes I detoured from my intended walk to check out another store. They offered me eggs, in boxes of six, on the shelf, but from caged birds. All the free-range eggs had sold. Reluctantly, I accepted them and took them home, feeling guilty.

6. Pop-Up People

22 April 2020

No. of UK cases: 4,310

Encouraged both by the weatherman's claim that the chill wind of recent days was easing, and by the continuing warm April sunshine, I walked across Pond Lane Recreation Ground. Dogwalkers were out as ever, but no children in their playground and no one at all on the grown-ups' 'playground'. What do you do with, or to, them – strange-looking pieces of Martian kit, or modern sculpture?

I looked across the Rec. to the tree-covered cone of Highdown Hill[8] and a National Trust property. It is quite a walk from hereabouts, but worth it for the good views it gives over the coastal plain from the Isle of Wight to Beachy Head and inland, and very popular with dogwalkers and anyone just wanting a breath of fresh air. There is history and interest there also, not least being Highdown Gardens[9] the gift to the town by Lady Stern of the chalkpit gardens she and her husband created. Nowadays it is closed not by Covid but, as intended some

---

8   Highdown Hill, https://en.wikipedia.org/w/index.php?title=High-down_Hill&oldid=994398068 (last visited 27 December 2021).

9   Highdown Gardens, https://highdowngardens.co.uk

months back, for a refurbishment project. The Gardens will be greatly missed this summer.

Sadly, the Rec. will not come alive with Durrington Festival Fair this June. Because of Covid, for the first time for 25 years it has been cancelled. The well-attended Saturday Fair is a lively occasion, with funfair, carnival procession and umpteen stalls. It will be missed, not just for the fun of the day but for the money and promotional value it provided to local charities, good causes and worthy organisations.

I took the footpath on the northern side of the church. Durrington and 'a church' are mentioned in the Domesday book but the church we see is little more than 100 years old. Its predecessor was partially demolished during the Civil War, when the parishioners were almost all Parliamentarians but their rector a Royalist. The church was not rebuilt and dedicated to St Symphorian[10] until 1915, by which time the village had begun to grow again.

With the church and the pub opposite both closed, I walked up through Vicarage Fields, not that the vicarage is there. The big tree I was looking for towered over the 1970s (or so) housing, and from it I followed the twitten leading up to the Arundel Road, the A27. No problem about crossing the A27 these days, so I turned into Cote Street. I walked up the rough, flinty unmade up road, with always interesting houses in variety on either side. From time to time, lovely views to Highdown opened up. Usually these have been across a shimmering river of traffic noise from the valley, but today the aural space was filled with birdsong.

---

10   Source for this paragraph: St Symphorian's Church, Durrington, https://en.wikipedia.org/w/index.php?title=St_Symphorian%27s_Church,_Durrington&oldid=1047804882 (last visited 21 December 2021).

At last, I heard footsteps behind me and turned to see a fellow-walker approaching. The pathway was wide enough for social distancing so I could enjoy passing the time of day with him safely. He then took the main path up to the open Downs above while I turned away and started to climb the other footpath to the right of the dividing chalkpit. That had been the meeting place of teenagers for a fag, a gossip and a giggle. The old rope hanging from an overhead branch on which they would idly swing and fool around was still there, so perhaps it has continued in use – even in Covid times, possibly? Luckily the spring growth of the woods had not yet overgrown the already narrow path. As I scrambled up between the chalkpit and the fence it was so narrow it would have been extremely difficult to pass at all, let alone keep to social distancing.

Fortunately, I did not meet another walker till the very end. Out into the sunshine, the open sky and the grassy fields. Plenty of wooden seats looked up to the sun expecting occupants, perhaps tired from picking sloes, with which the hedgerows abound in late summer, or just enjoying the view across to the Isle of Wight (weather permitting).

To my surprise, I saw some residents grouped at the corner of the road. But the much-loved and much-used shop had closed. Hadn't it? A pop-up shop had opened, or a new shop had popped up? mornings only, but it would be welcome news for friends living up here! It stocked an as-yet-limited range of foods. Milk and chocolate biscuits I saw; what else do you need? A little further on I stood at the gate of the 18th-century High Salvington Windmill.

I have a special interest here as I am one of the many volunteers who keep the old mill going. It is already over a month since I met my colleagues on Monday, 16 March for a regular morning's work that we took for granted. The Prime Minister's announcement that evening came as a shock. Our work was neither essential nor could we do it from home. A few days later came confirmation that the Mill, accordingly, would not be opening for the season in around a fortnight's time on 5 April. Right now, half a season's income, at least, would be lost, as was the case for most of the visitor attractions of Worthing.

The Mill's sails were set in the traditional diagonal St Andrew's cross but today, looking into the current north-easterly wind, were almost facing me down now, as an outsider. I could have gone down Mill Lane but, having had my fill of flinty unmade-up surfaces, I took the zig-zag path down to the Gallops. I have never seen horses galloping along this lengthy stretch of grass, but it provides a lovely sunny open view across to Cissbury Ring[11] and towards Chanctonbury Ring[12] on the horizon. Quite a few people around, quite a few dogs, a lot of space and the grassy slopes as white with daisies as if it had snowed.

The lower path outbound of the Gallops looked to be the path of choice into the woods so, contrariwise, I took the upper one. Immediately, I met a couple walking inbound. Very kindly they squeezed into and around a minuscule layby while I kept the path, and we discussed the etiquette required in such circumstances.

The path divided again, and again I took the one judged to be the less well travelled. In so doing I came across a big

---

11   National Trust, https://nationaltrust.org.uk/cissbury-ring

12   Chanctonbury Ring, https://en.wikipedia.org/w/index.php?title=Chanctonbury_Ring&oldid=1050219907 (last visited 21 December 2021).

tree on its side, but still flourishing. I guess this had come down in the 1987 hurricane! It was a chance to stand and enjoy the bluebells, patches of light here making shadows there, the pleasure of being warmed by the sun, the fresh damp smell of earth.

Back at the A27 I started to walk towards the pedestrian crossing, but why so? what would I be waiting for? A car? Yes, if I waited long enough, I would probably see one. If I were lucky, I might even see two, or even a lorry! In these topsy-turvy times, I crossed over forthwith! On a clear day you can see from the top of the hill the Rampion Wind Farm.[13] It brings home the height of the towers, as one is pretty much at eye-level hereabouts with the hub of the turbines. What I did see was the kindly act of a man trundling homeward the wheelie bin of a neighbour.

I stepped through to Half-Moon Lane; no pavements there but what does that matter these days? The half-moon curve that gives the lane its name is not all that apparent, and so back into Salvington from the north. I walked to the corner and *The John Selden* pub, named after the 17th-century polymath John Selden[14] born hereabouts in Salvington, then continued home past the silent playing fields of the school, and the little pond in its wild garden.

The weatherman was right. The wind had slackened, so warm enough for coffee in the garden, and a chocolate biscuit. And tonight, is the social event of the week, when I meet the neighbours for the NHS Clapping.

---

13 Rampion Wind Farm, https://en.wikipedia.org/w/index.php?title=Rampion_Wind_Farm&oldid=1052830395 (last visited 26 December 2021)

14 John Selden, https://en.wikipedia.org/w/index.php?title=John_Selden&oldid=1061113871 (last visited 21 December, 2021.

So that's lockdown. No one is going anywhere and there's nowhere to go, anyway. Next problem. How do we get out?

Relax!

from 13 May 2020

People may leave home for unlimited exercise and recreation. They can meet one person from another household in open air spaces but must keep two metres apart.

7. The New Etiquette

21 May 2020

No. of UK cases: 2,615

When lockdown began and social distancing was a phrase not well understood, I was uneasy about what would be the right thing to do when I met another person out on my walks, especially if I were to meet them in a narrow footpath. I tried to choose areas that were not the usual hotspots for visitors, but dogwalkers go everywhere. And, in accessing every park or green space I could possibly include, a narrow entry way was often incurred.

Thus, as I headed for Longcroft Park, my usual way out of the home area, someone came out of the footpath thereto and warned me that a family was coming. Indeed so, and I dutifully waited for them to come out before I went in. And they acknowledged my patience, and we were all cheered by the encounter.

Then I was walking through another development where the gardens backed onto wide paved twittens. I turned the corner to find two boys racing each other on scooters. The parents waved the boys to stop but they took no notice and sped towards me. And, without any sign of noticing my being there, divided around me as if I were a traffic island; one went one side, one the other. What's the problem?

Now, as lockdown has eased, what was concerning about footpaths in green areas has spread to the ordinary town pavement. It has become standard practice for one party to get out of the way to allow for two-metre separation. But standard pavements are a bare two metres wide. Only by hugging the wall on one side or balancing along the kerbstone on the other is 'social distance' maintained. But to force the other into such an awkward situation seems curiously ungracious, as if one is insisting on one's rights to the last millimetre.

So how to do the polite in the new normal of today? Sometimes by dodging into a gateway or other opening, or by stepping into the road, or indeed by crossing over. But who should make the manoeuvre, who should be the first to act; who has right of way? Clearly, we are aware of an approaching pedestrian early in the encounter. Working out all the details includes what would be the difficulties for the other person.

Who is more encumbered – by dogs on leads, shopping, children in pushchairs possibly with another small child as outrider on a scooter with no brakes? Have they the space to step into from the pavement – a grass verge or such? How dangerous is it to step into the road? Who would be facing the traffic, and who would have their backs to the traffic? What is the distribution of parked cars between us and them, behind which one can shelter from the traffic?

How late can one leave a decision? Will the other party be thinking along these lines at all? Will they recognise one's courtesy? Will there be a shy smile of recognition and thanks?

I, for one, have decided that if the oncomer is young they are unlikely to take action. If they are male and alone, they are unlikely to. And if they are young and male and alone, definitely not. So, coming down Durrington Hill, which has a pavement only on one side and that really narrow, I saw coming up a group of four to five teenagers – all from the same household? Who knows? – both boys and girls, and decided it would be prudent to cross the road at the junction with the next side road.

I could then loiter there until they had passed and then return safely to the pavement. Which I did, and was pleasantly surprised when they acknowledged this; firstly, the girl at the front of the group, followed by one or two of the others.

But it can get complicated. On the same walk, a man and family filled the pavement and were approaching. I did not want to cross over because there was no footway, the road was narrow, and the houses were right up to the road. So, I continued on, hoping to reach a road on my side before we all met. But they got there first. The man put out his arm to signal they were turning right, as we all used to do before cars had indicator lights. So, my turn to smile and thank.

And in the shops too, for all that there are markers here and guidelines there and 'no entry' signs, the moment comes when you do need to double back to change this or pick up that which was forgotten on the first transit. And so one squeezes into corners, or sidesteps rather than pass front-facing; an uneasy choreography plays out. But I am amused to note that, while the shop assistants and customers dance around each other at the two-metre distance, often enough when the shop staff talk to each other they close up to one metre.

In fact, I've noticed myself doing that with someone I know, such as my neighbour at the Thursday Clapping. With conjoined front paths and gates, it is difficult to stay the two metres away, so we tend to go onto the pavement. But, as we return to our houses, still talking to each other, the distance diminishes. You can *speak* to another person at two metres. If you want to *talk* with them, one metre is as much as we can manage.

And so, in these strange times a new etiquette has emerged. We do recognise the other's step as a courtesy. They have not stepped into the road by chance, or because they prefer walking on even roads than uneven pavements or want to look surprisingly closely at a prickly holly bush, but because they recognise, we recognise, that we share these same desires and need, and a have a responsibility to and for each other. And that's what makes us smile. It's not us and them. All are us.

from 1 June 2020

Six people can meet in a group outside, which includes private gardens.

8. The Call of the Wild

3 June 2020

It's too hot to go walking! So, walking has been confined to walking up and down the garden mowing the lawn, which takes about half an hour, and listening to the birdsong and bird calls. Not that I have many birds at all in the garden these days. Years ago, it was usual to have up to 16 little sparrows all sitting on the bough of the old apple tree chattering to each other while they waited their turn at the seed feeder.

But the bough rotted and fell. Then I put the food out on a round green plastic plate, which brought in larger birds. And, indeed, a seagull, which took not only the food but the plate as well! It flew off with this big round plate extending from its mouth like a flying platypus!

But increasingly the feeding process became dominated by pigeons and calling doves and the little birds left. I put the seed on a bird table with a roof over to prevent the bigger birds getting to the food, and their antics to do just that kept me amused. They succeeded, nevertheless. Nor did they confine their energies to the bird table. I had planted an amelanchier, a Canadian tree, that in the spring has lovely showy white flowers, and in the autumn enticing red berries. And so, the birds came and ate these until, finally, all that was left was a bunch of red berries at the outermost end of a light springy branch.

A fat pigeon flew in and sat on the branch at the stronger inner end, and looked at the tempting banquet. He moved his weight forward; the bough sprang up and down and he retired to safety. But temptation was too much: he lunged forward, the bough sagged, and he fell off! There is no doubt about it. He fell off! But he promptly spread his wings and arrived on the ground right way up.

Definitely looking a bit shaken and, I'm quite sure, rather self-conscious he shook himself about in a kind of 'Of course, I meant to do that' kind of way. 'Birds don't fall off. Of course not.' He flew back up to the branch to sit himself down in safe mode. The berries were still very tempting. So, he half-flew, half-walked to the end, and was duly rewarded.

However, the way the calling doves sat around calling to each other as they awaited a resupply of food annoyed me, especially when they sat on the chimneys. Their cries filtered down into the kitchen like repetitive ghostly voices.

I decided to stop feeding the birds, and also had spikes put around the chimneys. Now only the wind moves and twists in the chimney. A sound that those who live in modern houses never hear, which, on the whole, is a loss. But the calling doves have not gone away altogether. I became aware of this particularly one summer morn a year or two ago. A calling dove was sitting right by the house calling in a lugubrious tone 'To-day is now. To-day is now.'

This seemed a deep philosophical statement that had me worried. But got me out of bed.

Having got myself up and about, I then realised there was another calling dove elsewhere, saying, 'Bravo Kid. Bravo Kid.' This was much more encouraging. But the most vocal one, the most hard-working one, is the one who said, 'If you knew Suzy. If you knew Suzy.' He – she? – really worked at it, and I heard that call coming from all sides.

Sitting in the quiet of the evening garden, I look at the shaved lawn, almost a dustbowl, and question whether it is a good idea to cut the grass at all. And very occasionally, far away, I hear a distant cry, 'It's me. Suzy. It's me Suzy.' Will they ever meet up? Will true love blossom? Sadly, there's nothing I can do to help!

But I shall be meeting up in the near future with friends, for sure. Both are self-isolating or shielding for different reasons, so I am leaving it to them to set the rules and decide what we do. One is happy to go for a little walkabout and the other wants to sit and talk in the garden. It will be lovely to see them again. It will be nearly as great to see someone else's garden and watch another's grass grow.

9. Sunday Snips – A Monologue

6 June 2020

No. of UK cases: 1,557

There's a bit standing up there. I'll just give it a snip. Yes, that's good.

It just needs a little trim.

Oh, and can I reach that over there?

It's a bit long here, now I notice it.

It's got quite straggly. I'll just tidy it up.

How low and long it grows down there.

If I put my arm here and rest my elbow there; yes, I've got a hold.

Can't see really what I'm doing, but I think that's the bit?

Ouch! that was nearly my finger.

Anyway, I've done it now. Not sure that was where I meant.

How thick it grows. Maybe I can thin it out a bit.

I hope that doesn't show. But I'm not going to see it much; mostly.

Bit of a tangle there. Oh, was it meant to go that way?

Wonder if I should even it up a bit?

Oh dear, probably took off too much.

Not that it matters, I hope.

I think I can shape it better – there.

Just must stop.

So am I talking about cutting my hair or tidying up the garden shrubs? Does it matter? I use the same technique.

from 15 June 2020

Wearing a face covering on public transport becomes mandatory, unless exempt.

10. Braving the New Normal World

29 June 2020

No. of UK cases: 815

O h, the excitement! Oh, the joy! Standing at the petrol pump for the first time in three months. I'm going out! And about! In the meanwhile, though, the pumps have gone self-service. When we have to be social-distanced and Covid-secure for an indefinite time; that is right and proper. I must learn the trade.

I read the instructions and put in my credit card. The screen promptly rang up money. But I hadn't spent any! I'd barely got the pump out the holder! I found the cancel button. And tried again. It did the same thing. Was I being charged a deposit for their pump? But I could hardly drive off with it. The kindly motorist, patiently waiting his turn, came up and explained it did that, but all would be sorted once I had actually filled up.

Thus initiated into the new normal, I drove off into the sunshine, the space, big trees. The spring green of the early leaves as last seen had now become the heavy bluey-green of summer. I drove past the local PYO, its opening for the strawberry season one of the events that distinguished the rites and passage of the year. But, this year, the season of strawberries and cream is being celebrated not by Wimbledon but by the FA Cup semi-finals, with the Final itself still to come. Very odd. Only the daily Downing Street briefings have marked the passing days of lockdown and tolled the knell for many.

I was not going anywhere exciting, just to a click and collect depot. I walked across to the entrance, except that it now wasn't the entrance. An arrow on the glass pointed thataway. I walked on accordingly, and into the next entrance. That was now the exit. The staff member there gave directions to the new entrance, which I didn't understand, but it didn't matter because I saw the queue. I should, of course, have been looking for that as the great marker. There too was another staff member balancing with his colleague the numbers in and numbers out.

The queue wasn't too long, but everyone else was already furnished with trolleys. I hadn't seen those *en route* but didn't really need one. I took note, though, that my fellow queuesters, deeply engaged with their smartphones, were serious professionals, so no chat. In my amateurish way I just looked around. Lots of cars. At my neighbourhood shop at least we had the window of the charity shop to look at. After 12 weeks, I knew it by heart and progress along the pavement was marked by moving from the furniture to the books to the toys. It cheered us all up greatly when the window changed two weeks ago; the reopening was very welcome.

Inside, I joined the actual queue for click and collect, neatly marked out with blobs on the floor and arrows on the wall. In turn, I stepped into a booth between plastic screens. Across the barrier of trolleys, I offered the assistant the printout with all the details on. He looked surprised but came forward to take it. I then realised that the customers in the booths on either side were calling out the required numbers as given on the paperwork. However, he found my item and gave it me and returned my printout. I smiled, said 'thank you' and walked away, then thought, 'That was a bit old normal.' There was probably a button somewhere that, when pressed, would spring to life an emoji. Like.

On the way home I remembered the things I had meant to buy as well but forgotten and, in the interests of being Covid-secure, I should use the 'scan and shop' system. Accordingly, and in due course I picked up the appropriate handset. Nothing happened. No flashing lights on the screen. Something was wrong. A kindly shopper said in my ear, 'Have you registered?' and pointed towards a sort of letterbox. Pityingly, she took my loyalty card, held it under the letterbox, which beeped, and gave it me back. At least I didn't have to give my email and think of a password or answer questions to show I'm human; hopefully.

And so, I set forth. I needed some tomatoes. Pointed the handset at the barcode – nothing showed on the screen. I stretched out the plastic film to make it easier for the magic to happen – still it refused. A staff member passed by. I explained my problem and my beginner status. He promptly pointed the handset; the details showed on screen, and he commented I was probably holding the handset too close. How is it everyone else but me knows all these things? Weighing and packing loose fruit was for the Advanced Course, I reckoned. Not being ready for that, I moved on, and in due course finished up at the scan and shop checkout.

Promptly a sign came up saying the system wanted a manual check. Did it know it had a beginner here? I had in fact found it quite easy to forget to scan the items, too easy just throw them in the basket and walk on. The assistant came over and I was asked to stand in the corner – naturally – while she checked. It was good to go. I had passed! Did I get a certificate to say so? Only the bill.

So, contrary to my good intention, I had had probably more human contact in the course of these peregrinations than usual. The good news was that I had learned that my hairdresser is reopening next week. And that the staff had been on a course to ensure the salon was Covid-secure.

That, I thought, is what I need: a course! Meanwhile, it's 'learn on the job'.

11. Take-Off

9 July 2020

No. of UK cases: 704

To the hairdresser's! At last, after three months, I stood at the door halted, my arm outstretched. In old normal times I had just walked in and waited my turn on the comfy bench looking at magazines. Now, I was asked to wait outside! That explained why there were 2 or 3 people standing around. Or were they there for the other shops and establishments close by? It was all rather new. New also was that I had a face mask in my bag. *What's that? And what's it for? Why?* old normal me would have asked. But we all know why. It's living dangerously to go to the hairdresser's these days.

Turning my gaze outwards at the street, I found

there was enough to watch. A number of people walked past, and more were wearing masks than before. Indeed, as I stepped off the bus, where almost all were duly and dutifully wearing a mask, I had noticed how quickly some were taken off and packed away, others more slowly, or not at all.

There are different kinds of masks. As mine, the basic shop-bought mask, 10 in a pack. A bit of cloth whose concertina folds could open as required to suit the size of the face and its 3D contours, but otherwise dull. Then there was the homemade mask cut from a remnant of a much-loved piece of cloth, carefully shaped to suit the particular face of the wearer, or even 'boutique' style: patterned, coloured, the latest fashion in masks. And, finally, the technical mask. It probably came from work or hobby, like a gas mask without the goggles. I'm certainly not wearing one of those again.

At last, a customer came out. That was encouraging but, following instructions, I went on waiting. Then the stylist appeared in the doorway, but wearing what? It was not a mask. Masks cover the lower half of the face. They work from the bottom up, so that some are worn in a sort of half-mast, (half-mask?) position underslung below the chin, to be pulled up at the critical moment.

What the stylist had on was different. It covered all the face and was held up by something like a 1920s' head band. A top-down system. Is it a visor? In the days of old, a knight in shining armour wore a helmet to protect his whole head from the charging enemy, while a metal visor when raised gave full vision, or closed gave minimal eye space. Surely, this was in that knightly tradition as the whole face was protected. Yet eyes were here visible at all times, through a see-through rigid half-circle of plastic.

A modern solution for a modern problem, the invisible enemy; and for a body shield a plastic pinny.

And there's a cultural difference. Visors are for knights – the good guys who raise fear in the enemy's hearts. Masks not only hide people's faces they conceal identity. So baddies wear them. Or you go to a masked ball to feel free to choose your identity. Or, with a cult, the priests wear a headdress to identify with the deity and impress the supplicants as they lead the rites and may speak from echoing chambers to magnify their power. Who, which, was I following in?

As I fumbled belatedly to put on my mask, I realised I was to be initiated into the rituals. These we shall grow used to. I must cleanse myself, or at least my hands, with sanitiser first and only then divest myself of my outdoor coat onto the designated stand. I followed along the prescribed path and took my seat. It was separated from the other chairs by plastic screens that gave each a good metre of room. In my own space in my own stall, I was cloaked in my own plastic pinny, plus the usual barber's big coverall. Then my chair was raised to working height. Thus, installed, enrobed and enthroned, I became a junior member of the collegiate. I was in with the good guys!

And so, to the usual opening address, 'What would I like done?' Years before I had been to the hairdresser of the time, and as she ran her comb through my hair had asked, disdainfully, 'Have you been cutting your hair, madam?' Not having any alternative, I confessed my sin, and she graciously accepted my penitence and redeemed the damage. At least, on this occasion, hairdressers know what awaits them, and my stylist made no comment on my overgrown hair (on one side) and overcut hair (on the other).

According to the instructions, there was to be no conversation after the initial formalities. But questions like 'How am I? How have I managed?' etc. do not expect a reply detailing every ache or every problem so are both formal and friendly human. Thereafter silence followed. It gave space to contemplate the rhythmic rise and fall of comb and scissors as they progressed around my head: robotic, hypnotic, entrancing. The final conversation broke the spell, 'Was that enough? Did I want more off?' and the last act of traditional magic: seeing the back of my own head. *Lovely, lovely!* The stylist too shared in this Looking Glass World for the procedures forbade any approach from the front.

I had been absolved of my superfluous hair. I certainly felt the better for that. But what kind of better? Not physical/medical. Not religious/spiritual, but in some way, I had been ennobled? Arise, milady! But I was brought back down to earth in every sense.

While the stylist briefly returned to the Cinderella role of sweeping away the detritus of my hair and binning the coverings, I moved to the paydesk in its own screen-wrapped world. I hovered my card above modern magic. There has long been talk about the cashless society and it becomes ever more real with Covid. I still have most of the cash drawn just before lockdown.

Outside, in the freedom once more of a well cut head of hair I took off my mask thankful to my knight in plastic visor who had rescued this damsel in distress! Snippings of hair floated away, reminders of battle. As I said, it's living dangerously to go to the barber's!

12. South to the Sea

16 July 2020

No. of UK cases: 642

I thought, 'I'm running out of things to do! I could sort out the back bedroom, empty the garage or find out what is in the big heavy suitcase under the bed. But apart from that I haven't anything much to do. There's the washing-up, of course, but there's always the washing-up. I'll just have another coffee... Not sure if I'm suffering from claustrophobia or agoraphobia; cribbed and confined by cabin fever but having neither the energy nor the will to do much about it. Let me be a daytripper to Worthing.'

And so, with a café cum takeaway in prospect, walking the longish route was an option. I headed out firstly for Northbrook College's grounds at the very edge of Worthing. Highdown Hill loomed to the north; and westwards stretched fields with maturing wheat (and dogwalkers around the edge). This took me down past hedges of brambles and a tree of little red apples onto Goring Station. A train went through at the very moment I arrived, so the barriers were down. Eight coaches, eight passengers as far as I could see, one of them certainly wearing a face mask.

From there down through an avenue of trees created by the gentryfolk who also built and lived at Goring Hall[15] and placed it at the centre of a crossroads of such wooded avenues. And behold, the Sea! the Wind! the Sky! And the spaciousness of it all. I was standing on the beach edge with nothing but nothing ahead, if not quite all around me. A few other people were doing much the same. A good sprinkling of groups and couples sitting on the beach but plenty of room available midweek, and quiet too.

We were all in the same mood; not taking it all for granted, not regarding the greensward or the beach as the place to hold a barbecue, or dance around to noisy music, or kick a ball about, but aware of the joy and pleasure in its own right of being out, of not being inside walls and in rooms lumbered with furniture, not having our eyesight impeded by houses and roads and concrete and brick, nor even fences and hedges, woods and trees, nor looking across empty silent streets to unchanging walls opposite.

Just sea and air, of which there was plenty. In the knockabout wind, the leaves of big trees oscillated between silver grey and green as the tormented branches struggled to keep steady. Anything that could move the scouring wind shifted, or it pitted itself against anything that would not. One small tent, plump with wind, was at the point of vertical lift-off until the owner added a couple more weights to hold it down. Another would rather have spent the day at Beachy Head[16] at the very edge of the eastern horizon, so its owner took it down altogether. A cleansing

---

15   Goring Hall, https://historicengland.org.uk/listing/the-list/
      list-entry/1250827/?section=official-listing.

16   Beachy Head, https://beachyhead.org.uk.

wind that blew away all the cobwebs and the fustiness gathered inside the weeks of lockdown. The kitesurfers were taking full advantage of the wind; their beautiful parabolas of colours and patterns sweeping back and forth over the turquoise sea. Their sailors, brushing their way through the water, cast off white spume each side of their minimal craft.

I bought a coffee and a sausage roll from the café-cum-takeaway. A big marquee was ready to offer shelter but I would not allow even that to cut me off from the wide horizon. A shadow rippled over the pebbles. A seagull landed. Its cruel eye glared, unblinking, at my sausage roll. Its supercilious beak curled in anticipation. Its social distance closed from two metres to one-metre-plus, to one-metre-minus. Undaunted, I left not a crumb. It flew off. For such a noisy bird its colours, grey, white and a touch of black I noted, are surprisingly muted, the colours of the sea on a misty morning, under a leaden sky.

The pebble beach stretched endlessly before us east and west. Why are our beach pebbles largely brown and white when on the Downs, and in the gardens, they are so often grey and black? I believe it is because the beach pebbles have worked their way up the coast from the red earth of Devon. Pebbles may be a pain to walk on, though we locals learn at an early age the art of sideslipping the feet into them, but they make for a lively scene.

When changing handbag for daysac, I had run through the check list: money, keys, phone, bus pass – but had forgotten the new piece of kit we now have to carry: a face mask. I would need to walk back. I pointed my feet in the right direction up Sea Lane Goring. Trying to recall the 4 other 'Sea Lanes' of the locality occupied my mind until, in due course, I heard the glad sound of a kettle boiling. Home again and feeling much refreshed for my day out down by the sea.

13. Back on Board

30 July 2020

No. of UK cases: 846

Some time back, in old normal days, I joined the group waiting at the bus stop. That there was a group was alarming in itself. The bus was supposed to run every 10 minutes, which scarcely gave time for any build-up. Ours is a humble bus stop. We do not have the electronic display boards found at important bus stops in important shopping areas: the boards where time stands still, or even goes backwards.

Minutes came and went but no bus. Discussion of the weather turned to the absentee bus. We may be fortunate to have such a good service but still complain when it doesn't happen. We came out with the usual phrases, 'It says on average; that means six an hour – all at once?' The consensus was that no one had ever met six buses coming at the same time, the most being three, which was, I suppose, encouraging. Sometime later I told this tale to my brother-in-law, who used to drive buses. He looked away and sighed deeply, remembering his struggles to get the bus round the course on time.

However, while these reminiscences drew us altogether as bus stop buddies, the young man standing apart and aloof and listening to sounds not directly available to the human ear, came alive. He tapped his phone in sequence and announced the bus would be here in three minutes. Full of wonder at this news from on high and amazed at his command of such rituals, we waited expectantly. And, indeed, three minutes or so later the bus made its way up the hill and turned the corner to our bus stop. For us technological peasants: awesome!

And so, today, having heard that the bus in these Covid times was running at 30-minute intervals, I sought such wonder powers for myself. In other words, I downloaded the bus app, a phrase that a few years back would have seemed total nonsense but now merely demands knowledge of certain rites and practices; which was the problem. I headed into the magic world with the confidence of the Sorcerer's Apprentice. I worked on the advice given by a friend years back: if you don't know the answer but are expected to, just say yes and no alternately.

Lo and behold, I had before me the timetable – for East Kent! By devious means, I found my way back through the maze to West Sussex. An abstract arrangement of coloured lollipops filled the screen. Interesting! Then I recognised them as the bus stops around here, and, yes, that one with its head filled in was *my* bus stop! And as I scrolled down came the bus times themselves. Success!

I realised it was offering the old Saturday service, five buses an hour. What a great number 60 is, divisible by 2, 3 and 5! That was credible and good news, so I ventured forth. And, more or less as stated, the bus came along. Our humble bus stop does have a shelter of sorts, which gives some protection, but, problematically, it is placed central to the marked bus space, so you have to guess at which end the bus will pull up. Further, the bus space tends to be closed off quite sharply by parked cars, so the driver has to judge his angle of exit. And that determines whether the first or last in the queue gets the break.

However, it is not always a blessing to be at the right end of the shelter. For the customer, meanwhile, also has to judge, as the bus swings in to the pavement, whether, where and to what extent the wheel cover is going to swing over the pavement and if withdrawal from one's prime position is a wise precaution. And sometimes the bus just stops well away from the kerb altogether, which makes the step on board quite high.

All this, of course, while getting one's bus pass out and ready to show. So now in Covid times is added the moment when you need to fix your face mask. My preliminary thoughts on this had left me to decide to fix it from ear to ear fairly early on, but not to draw it up over my mouth and nose until the moment I stepped on board. The routine then is: bus pass in one hand; cover face; pick up shopping. Hope I don't need a third hand to haul myself onto bus.

So, having passed the entrance exam and said 'hallo' to the driver, one is allowed into the bus proper. And to choose one's seat. There is a certain order, I think, in one's priorities bearing in mind the distance one is travelling and whether the bus is double-decker or single. Short distance to sit downstairs; long-distance and not too loaded: go upstairs. Or short distance sit at the front; longer at the back. That can be pre-determined, perhaps, before entering.

But where is the particular seat you will head for? A quick survey must then gauge how full the bus is. Most of us would rather choose a seat to ourselves – is that still possible? If not available, men would rather sit with men and women with women, I have observed. All of which is complicated by there not being a standard bus layout. And to this the requirements of social distancing are now added.

The very first seat is cordoned off. Is it better to pass everyone to head for the back, or sit in a frontish seat and have everyone pass you? How does social distancing apply hereafter? As the bus lurched off fairly quickly and swung round the corner, I headed for a single seat in the front, which seemed a reasonable distance from her, two rows back on my side, and also from him, one row back on the other side. I had chosen well, as I could now read the instructions on the noticeboard on what to do, which are otherwise not easily read. Currently double seats should be occupied by either one person or one household, and one should leave a row between oneself and another.

So I was mildly annoyed when, at the next stop, a woman got on who promptly sat directly behind me. She wouldn't even have been able to read the instructions from there. And was wearing a very odd mask. Homemade, interesting material, probably a leftover from curtains, but it covered only her mouth. If you had to choose, surely you should cover your nose? People came on and got off. Men and women, all wearing masks. We pulled up at a busy stop. Two women – mask free – came on and showed some authorisation to the driver. In the smart modern way, they held up their mobile phones to him, nothing old hat like a piece of paper. I had noticed them as the queue trudged its way into the bus and reckoned they needed to lip read.

Then a man and his son came on. The son was, I would say, over the age when masks are required but neither he nor his father were wearing any such. They showed no paperwork in support, and the driver made no effort, as far as I could see, to query this. A bus driver is not in the position of a coach driver, who, far more, is the captain of the ship and what he says goes. It is public perception that has the power and so a relief to see that virtually everyone was masked.

I sat dreamily looking out the window and saw the most marvellous parasol parading majestically down the street. I guess it had an Asian origin, such was the rich mix of colours and patterns glittering with silver in the sunshine, tassels swaying in time with the stately progress of its owner. Is there a face mask to match, I wonder? That would be worth wearing!

But an imminent problem presented. The sudden but welcome dose of summer sunshine had brought on a touch of hay fever. My nose needed attention. I brought out my handkerchief. Now what to do?

14. Day Tripper (Part 1)

5 August 2020 (am)

No. of UK cases: 892

I suffer badly from cabin fever! It occurs at the most inconvenient times, such as the dead of winter or, as now, in the Covid lockdown. Fortunately, I am at home so know how to deal with it. There is no absolute cure, it is a recurring problem, but one can get and take various items to alleviate the symptoms. Accordingly, I got out my daysac and took the train.

There is a saying, 'He goes farthest who knows not whither he is going'. It probably means if you don't know where you're going you just go round in circles and take a long time to get nowhere. But I hope there is a more optimistic reading, namely that if you have a specific goal, you stop when you have achieved it, whereas if you have a more open-ended approach you will achieve more. On that principle I set forth with Plan A (provisional) in mind. Where indeed to go in these Covid times? I felt the need to be cautious but surely, we can apply some cunning to that caution. And decided the best solution was to go where I could be outdoors as much as possible.

Having seen from time to time that the Coastway trains had almost more carriages than people on board, that seemed the mode of transport to take. Indeed so: there was only one other person in my carriage. The train chuntered along through the summer Sussex countryside as the Downs retreated to an edge of the northern horizon and dark blue-green trees hedged the golden stubble left from the corn harvest. The train tiptoed carefully across the Arun river, treading lightly onto one track and off that onto another, then moved into its stride. It passed umpteen glasshouses whited out with sheets and whitewash which matched, on the other side of the track, arrays of black solar panels, the latest growth industry, if growth is appropriate. The silvery cap of Halnaker windmill flashed as the sunlight caught it, more like a lighthouse.

After the elegant spire of Chichester Cathedral, the train rumbled on through the back streets and passed equally scruffy fields of paddocks and aimless horses and unused machinery. The purpose of trains is to join up towns and people; the purpose of motorways is to avoid them at all costs. But, whichever, the graffiti boys get there too. How do they do it? In the middle of nowhere some rail-required blockhouse stands close to the line yet has graffiti on it. After all that effort, it's just a pity their skills and abilities do not extend to the graffiti itself.

And so, to the Victorian splendour of Portsmouth & Southsea railway station, surrounded by giants of glass and steel and indeed colours too, black glass or cladding and orange framed window shapes. And on to the wondrous edifice of the Spinnaker Tower, one of the most exciting pieces of public architecture and sculpture around. Not that I am going up it. Ever! I learned early on that I do not have a head for heights.

I traipsed after a small group at the Harbour station down the tunnel to Wightlink [17] Ferries' quayside, notices on all sides about Covid care and instructions of where to go and what to do. I stood on the outside jetty thinking to be near the entry point onto the catamaran itself. So, a chance to look around the harbour – the Gosport ferry on its never-ending crossing of the harbour. A red tug covered in black tyres punched its way outbound against the waves and the tide. The marina opposite full of tall masts and a few sailboats preparing for action.

The catamaran from Ryde turned up on cue and berthed a little way up our jetty. Passengers got off. A crewman came to the barrier between and the dozen of us came alert in expectation that he would take it down. Instead, he added to it the barrier from the inner doorway and those in the inside waiting area took their chance. Having thus altered the order of accession I had imagined (as so often happens), we followed on, and on with the mask. It was a very controlled entry in groups to allow people to disperse around the craft as they wished before another group came on board to do the same.

My principle of being outdoors failed when I realised that out on the sundeck one would be facing into the brisk wind of the day, increased by the speed of the vessel itself. I headed for the forward indoor area and took a seat right by the open entrance for the crew onto the foredeck. There was plenty of space around for the few passengers compared with the capacity of the saloon. We lumped and bumped away across the Spithead[18] channel: just enough contact with the sea to realise that that was where we

---

17   Wightlink Isle of Wight Ferries, https://www.wightlink.co.uk/
18   Spithead, https://en.wikipedia.org/w/index.php?title=Spit-head&oldid=1053537310 (last visited 21 December 2021).

were. A huge great cruise ship with its umpteen layers of decks was on the horizon inbound.

With the ship berthed at Ryde pier we made ready to disembark, but they had their plan for us. Passengers were to disembark in order according to the colour code of their seats. But all the seats are the same colour, dark blue? Oh no: the end seat of each row had a colour sticker on it. That was why I couldn't see it. My back was resting on it!

The little old Tube train took us down the long pier. I was glad that the ticket clerk at my station had advised me so to do. It's a long walk otherwise. I looked around the shops and the visitors sparsely scattered along the front and on the pleasant greensward on the seaward side: a good place for a picnic or for eating fish and chips.

I wanted something traditional and local but hopefully a bit better than fish and chips and walked up the hill looking for an outdoor eating area, and in and out of a couple of restaurants. One too noisy and one the service too slow. I looked into another, ready prepared for guests having at the door both sanitiser and the Test and Trace form, but it had no outdoor capacity.

I finally found a table in the shade outdoors, though surrounded by the back side of tall blocks of flats. My traditional ploughman's lunch was promptly delivered full of good food and nutrition and very welcome was the good coffee.

As I paid the barman – all and only me paying as (too late) I had chosen a restaurant not sharing the Chancellor's bounty – he indicated a Test and Trace gadget. It offered the QR (Quick Response) system. It was so unexpected in its modernity I was nonplussed on both theoretical and practical grounds. Is this part of some Isle of Wight trial system yet to be applied to the mainland? What information is going in and to whom? Do you need a special QR app to zap it with, or does the ordinary phone camera suffice?

In any case, I need 10 minutes notice for such things. My phone lies at the bottom of my bag and takes forever to come to life. There was no paper form alternative to hand, but completion is, for the time being, voluntary, and I was now in a hurry to catch the ferry. And so, feeling somewhat guilty at my non-compliance, I headed back for Portsmouth. This time I took a seat on the sun deck, so no mask required, and with the afternoon still to enjoy.

15. Day Tripper (Part 2)

5 August 2020 (pm)

No. of UK cases: 892

The steep hills over which Ryde is spread grew smaller as the catamaran pulled away so that one saw the town as one piece. Many dark green trees separated some fine public buildings. The skyline was pierced by the tall spires of two churches as, in Italy, tall poplars or cypresses separate houses and buildings. But why was so much of the town plastered in white or dirty cream? Why not some Italian colour – soft pastels, blues and greens and pinks?

I walked up from the ferry terminal at Portsmouth Harbour station to take the underpass through to Gunwharf Quays shopping. Such a different world from Ryde. I had felt ahead of the times there (mostly). Here I felt way behind. Big shopwindows full of enlightening, enticing, exciting displays!! A pleasant number of people around gave the buzz that a crowd provides but not in such intensity to feel endangered by the numbers. Plenty of people at the umpteen eateries with their large outdoor spaces. Lots of signs and notices around: on the ground for one-way walking; on the walls and doors the requirements for face masks. One notice stood out: *Do not attach bicycles to these railings. They will be removed.* Surely easier to remove the bicycles?

A few short queues outside shops. The longest queue was, of course, for the toilets, where a guardian clicked and controlled numbers for both sexes. Quite a few sanitiser stops throughout the centre, like drinks stands for marathon runners.

The sun was warmer, the clouds and wind less as the boat for the harbour tour reversed out almost right under the ribs of the Spinnaker Tower. The storytelling began. Was I sitting comfortably? Not greatly! I had taken to the sundeck where the container boxes for lifejackets did the job of seating. However, we were sitting safely, outside, in the sunshine, more or less the right distance from others and masks not really required.

The words and pictures, sounds and sights flowed together as we toured the harbour and its history, ranging from naval to commercial to leisure. We floated among the old and the new, the very big and complex and the small and simple. How small HMS *Victory* and HMS *Warrior* looked compared with the latest biggest ships to join the Royal Navy, the aircraft carriers HMS *Queen Elizabeth* and HMS *Prince of Wales*! What strange shapes some ships now take, curiously angular and with strange structures, obelisks for this and globules elsewhere for that! How big the cruise liner in the commercial port looked compared with the yachts of the marina nearby! Buoyed up by seeing a world edged by land, we returned to our berth, and I stepped back onto a world edged by water.

Time to head for home. The boats and ships' theme of the day had one last outing. A sequence of pylons stretched like ships of the line over the harvest fields. I see them as in the tradition of 'Quinqueremes from Nineveh from distant Ophir',[19] with giant arms rowing themselves across the land or, as the latest in the Silk Road tradition. Like ungainly camels they stalk stiff-legged over the countryside to download their swag in the warehouses of power.

I was glad to be home. Had I enjoyed the day? It was nice to be out, but not carefree as in normal times. Nothing much was spontaneous or left to chance. They had a plan already for you, which was both reassuring but also alarming. I had felt on edge all the time. Judging distance between people. Avoiding one lot here, wary of that lot there. Watching what they're doing. Checking notices on the floor. Seeing reminders on the walls. Putting on a mask here; maybe not needing it there, possibly. What I was grappling with is the realisation that this state of affairs is what we have to get used to, and it does take some getting used to. And the more we do it, the more streetwise we become.

Perhaps on one's home turf the drill has become customary and a routine one feels safe with has been established. One is reasonably confident that most everyone is going to be doing the right thing. But 'out of area': will that still be the case? Indeed, it is. For almost everyone has much the same concern and almost everyone was wearing masks as required, on the trains, in the ferries, around the shopping centre and, of course, in the toilets. One person needed to be reminded by a warden to put on their mask before entry. There's always someone! And that someone was me!

Have I cured the current bout of cabin fever? For the time being maybe. But I still have itchy feet and an idea for going just a little further…

---

19 'Cargoes', https://www.public-domain-poetry.com/john-mase-field/cargoes-3049.

from 8 August

Wearing a face covering becomes mandatory in indoor settings such as museums and cinemas, unless exempt.

16. Home and Away

21 August 2020

No. of UK cases: 1,089

I sighed with relief and happiness as I sank into my accustomed chair. Home again! Home into my preferred seat in many years of happy coach travel with Worthing Coaches[20]. It had been a long time since I had sat there. I told a friend a few days ago that I was going on this trip, and he thought I was very brave! No one thought that when I last climbed aboard almost six months ago, for a trip to London and a tour of the Royal Opera House. No need then to have our foreheads tested for temperature checks, no need for an on-board hand sanitiser dispenser, no need then to wear face masks on board. And our lunch together and visit around the Opera House itself would now contravene every nuance of social distancing.

Over that weekend, also, my friend in Australia had telephoned, doubtful about his planned trip to UK for

---

20   Worthing Coaches, https://www.worthing-coaches.co.uk/

the summer. He was already concerned about coronavirus both in Australia and UK. But his airline company was in no mood to reimburse his fare if he cancelled. That same weekend the first published UK hospital admissions for coronavirus came as 51 people were admitted to hospital for that reason, and by the end of the first week of March the total number of confirmed cases had risen to 200. I realised a planned lunch gathering might be the last for some time, 'Social distancing' had entered our vocabulary. There was talk of three months self-isolating. Everyone was stocking up not quite sure what for. Then came the announcement on 16 March closing in on almost everything, ASAP.

I took a last load of garden rubbish to the recycling centre. A visit to the hairdresser and as I left, I said, 'See you in a month.' Neither I nor they were convinced. A final meeting of an exercise group. Everyone was looking for toilet rolls, but I was searching for eggs. And at the Downing Street briefing of Friday 20 March, time was called. Pubs were to close forthwith. But the sun shone on Sunday for the best weather we had had after Storm Ciara, Storm Dennis and Storm Jorge all but drowned us. Who could stay home? I headed for the park and the beach beyond. It was warm. It was sunny. It was lovely.

I extended my walk to the pier and met a couple of friends, in the same mood. At a coffee kiosk, customers were being kept at bay by a barricade of tables and I too was getting edgy. There were too many people too close, closer than this magic number of two metres that we now had to live with. I headed home for lunch. The bad news was that the total number of confirmed cases was now around 6,000. Lockdown came in the next day, 23 March. As I have reported, buses and trains ran empty. The streets filled with silent, unmoving cars.

I was so glad to feel the movement of the coach slow, and then turn into Clacket Lane Service Station. It has always encouraged me that here I was away, at last, for the day. Two HGVs against all the rules were in the coach bays. Amazingly we were the only coach there. Even more amazingly, there was no queue at the ladies'. A lengthy web of marked passages led to my chosen coffee bar. I walked quickly through and at the exit the *maitre d'* (as he would have been called in a grander establishment) greeted me and pointed to screens. I tapped as directed. No success. A long tap? No, press and hold? No. The *maitre d'* showed me the coffee bar tap – short, light, quick and one-fingered. 'Contactless preferred.' The cash I had drawn mid-March stayed again in my purse. I collected the coffee from the servery and took it round to the grassy area outside, the air slightly damping and mizzling, but no bother. I was definitely away. Hurray!

The M25 continued running along the south side of the North Downs a little longer, then we climbed over to the north side and the M2 before breaking away again to the A299. Glimpses of the sea and the foreshore on our left. Oh yes, we're off to Margate. I had been there umpteen years before with the family. It had rained all week, but I did learn to drive the family car there. Apart from that, I had no memory of the town. But Margate's Information Centre was well marked with big banners outside, and gave me an excellent map and handy information, as below.

I walked up the hill past the sign that proudly proclaimed Margate as Britain's first seaside resort in 1736, to look for the Saxon fire beacon: a tenet, which gives the district its name, Thanet. Couldn't find it. I walked to the Margate Caves. Closed. And into the Old Town. The

Tudor House. Closed. The historic Cobbs Pub. Closed. Was it just Monday, the end of season feeling, or had they just not opened at all this year? I did find Alkali Row, where they burned seaweed to an ash to send to Holland for the glazing of Delft Pottery. Maybe Worthing has the wrong kind of seaweed. Back on the seafront to the seafood stall for a crab sandwich. Had run out!

Partly at the Chancellor's expense (thank you, Mr Sunak), I enjoyed a good lunch on the umbrellaed terrace and looked across the sandy beach. And so, at last, there was what I had come for. The sea in the wrong place, in the north! It sparkles differently as a result, but sparkly it certainly was. Freighters and container ships crawled along the dark ribbon of the horizon until closed from view by the curtain of clouds.

I took my coffee in hand and headed for the end of the short pier. I passed the Turner Contemporary Gallery (closed). And so, sitting here I could now look southwards, across the sea to the land and the sun twinkling in and out the white clouds. The wind was pleasant, warmed by all the land it had crossed since the English Channel. An interesting townscape to behold. Some pastel shaded houses flanked either side by Victorian red brick. A deep bay with wide sandy beach and families making the most of the space and the sun.

The day was beginning to turn and the silhouette figures on the beach began the packing-up ritual: folding up the wind break, rolling the beach mat, struggling with the traditional deck chair in the traditional way, picking up the cool box, the spades and the buckets. The sea had moved away from the beach, the small yachts and boats were resting on their bilge keels. A couple of larger yachts rested against the seawall.

The memorial clock tolled the hour in the most musical tone I have ever heard. The coach came in on time and we donned our face masks and climbed aboard. Social distancing as now practised on the coach had one great benefit: with the numbers limited and the inner seat on the driver's side out of bounds, I was guaranteed a double seat all to myself! A smooth journey home without stopping. We came south down the A23 as far and as long as we could, only to turn away when we reached the shimmering lights of Brighton Palace Pier.

The sea, back in its accustomed place south of us, was a malevolent deep green under the evening sky, and choppy with a few white horses. A dark uniform cloud had taken out most of the light, but to the west the horizon was alight. The journey is not yet over, but that, hopefully, is where we're going.

17. In The Lee

1 September 2020

No. of UK cases: 1,295

With the tea made and mug in hand, I walked across the wood laminate floor of my temporary domain and looked out into the late summer sunshine. Mostly, I could see the neighbouring wood-log walls of the next lodge. But a huge weeping willow also dominated, towering like a green cumulus over a stream that cut its way unseen between untidy hedges. A blue jay winked its eye at me, almost lost among the long, lush grass, large docks, giant cow-parsley and wildly growing plantains. This area had more water than my sparsely growing garden could dream of.

The journey had gone well. Alone in my carriage on the London bound train, it seemed safe to release my face mask. Even at Gatwick no one disturbed my peace; in fact, almost no one disturbed any peace on any platform. That was disturbing in itself! I changed trains, and with time to spare decided to go into the terminal. I was shocked. Only the pharmacy and one coffee bar were open. Only North

Terminal was in use. Only when the shuttle from there disgorged a few passengers was there any life in the place. I had noticed in a bemused way, as the train drew into the station, the long line of colourful aircraft tailfins. Now the reason was obvious. There weren't any passengers. Or, to put it t'other way round: Gatwick is now a parking lot for unwanted aircraft.

The train drew into London Bridge station. My memory of it from years back was as the dreariest of the London south coast stations. So different now. All glass and steel and long escalators and smart shops and wide concourses, but still recognisable and comforting was the Victorian solid underpinning of red-brick arches. So different now was the view itself as I walked over London Bridge. The Shard, the Gherkin, the Cheesegrater and other amazing edifices of shining silvery glass that reflected into each other in a narcissistic way: look at me, looking at you. But in one was mirrored St Paul's Cathedral, a reminder that history lasts a long time and may have different values.

It had not been a good idea to walk. At the foot of the shiny silvery deep canyons that Gracechurch Street and Bishopsgate had now become, the air was filthy. Covid-19 was the least to worry about. I was lucky that the train from Liverpool Street Station was almost waiting for me to arrive and then set off. The train sped out past rows of neat Victorian terraces and chaotic modern industrial developments to its first stop, at Tottenham Hale. Flat grassy areas and narrow rivers and even narrower boats. Another 10 minutes and the train stopped again. The country air of the Lee Valley was so fresh and clear and clean after London's stink only 20 minutes away. I walked to my accommodation, YHA Lee Valley.[21]

---

21   Youth Hostels Association, https://www.yha.org.uk

Some seven years previously, in September 2013, I had been taken on an interesting London walk from the southern end of the Lee Valley. We had walked the Limehouse Cut up to the tidal mills at Three Mills Island and the Olympic Park, then across unexpected marshlands before stopping to see the Markham Steam Beam Engine[22] at Tottenham. Now I wanted to go further upstream to the River Lee Country Park, the six miles or so from Waltham Cross northwards to Broxbourne.

My accommodation was self-catering as I had decided that would be safer than 'catered for'. But it would be real self-sufficient self-catering as the kitchen (for all residents of the lodge) was firmly out of use. The shelves were empty of china, the worktop was bereft of kettles, and the cupboards below bare of pots and pans. All as Covid security required, but so contrary to the sharing and friendliness that was at the heart of my YHA experience. Hot drinks were available from Reception, but I thought I could manage with my little travelling jug that I had purchased years back at a 'bring and buy' stall for 50p! It would be more like self-catering B&B, but it is surprising what there is these days that just needs hot water! Obviously, it would be much easier, therefore, if travelling by car as other groups were in other lodges. After an evening wander by the canal and a morning 'continental' style breakfast – wishing I had a tray to take breakfast to a picnic table outside – I set out for the day. While passing through central reception (and duly wearing a facemask), I noticed that the board of tourist information had also been removed for Covid security reasons.

I stepped out of the train at Broxbourne, a pinchpoint where canals and river meet, and they built the railway

22 Markham Steam Beam Engine, https://www.mbeam.org.

hereabouts also. The result is a spaghetti junction of footpaths, foot bridges, underpasses, roads, road bridges and carparks. Most of these I traversed as I went the long way, wrong way, round heading for the café set among the watermeadows. It is a five minutes' walk from the station, when you know how.

My purpose was not so much the thriving takeaway that the café (with organised social distancing) had now become though its priority was increasing, but to walk among the water meadows. I stepped out along the duckboard path into an 'Everglades' situation. So much water is there that the roots of trees that once thrived are now drowned, and the trees rise like skeletons above the green algae-filled waters. At sight of me, two white swans cut a path through the green surface heading for any food I might carry, but I kept walking. Outside, the trees were still in the full green leaf of summer but here, the leaves on what was not already dead, were yellow ghosts of former lives.

The path turned back as a gravel path on firm land and the trees also returned to life. I passed the remains of Broxbourne Water Mill mentioned in the Domesday Book,[23] its water wheel idle as I passed by.

I had seen along the canal narrow boats neatly tied up, making use of all of a town's advantages, easy access to shops, supermarkets. But just over a mile downstream it was not the same. Beside the canal path the water flowed quietly and seeming gently. The moorhens, mallards and coots and occasional swans seemed not bothered whether they moved upstream or downstream. But where canal and river separated at the King's Weir, it was startling to see the force of water dropping over the cill and seething

---

23 Broxbourne Mill, https://en.wikipedia.org/w/index.php?title=Brox-bourne_Mill&oldid=1031724366 (last visited Dec. 21st 2021)

in coffee-coloured foam as it struck the lower waters. Nearby sat a hopeful, patient fisherman under his large umbrella.

For hereabouts was what nature did when left to itself. It grew. Hereabouts was the choice on how to reach the southern end of the park, if that's what you wanted to do. The efficient way was to take the gravel towpath alongside the canal. The alternative was not. With both OS. 174 'Epping Forest and Lee Valley' in hand and the excellent free leaflet 'Acres of Fun' produced by the Lee Valley Regional Park Authority,[24] I spent a couple of happy days doing both, working my way haphazardly southwards. The leaflet shows umpteen paths, both the man-made gravel path (such as the towpath) or the natural grassy tracks.

The canal and towpath have their own interests and it was sufficient just to see the variety of narrowboats and their owners who travel. And a surprising number were single-handed – a lot of work and effort for one person to get through a lock.

The view from the towpath can be limited by the wall of bullrushes and sedges that spread away from the path or line the other side of the canal. But glimpses of lakes and pools of differing sizes are seen beyond. In that wilder world, paths lead to viewpoints and also the hides, though the hides themselves were shut in the name of Covid security. Across the spread of Holyfield Lake some swans, in fright at seeing a person edging their territory, began their take-off but noisily aborted it and continued feeding and grooming as they quickly realised I was harmless.

Away from the towpath, double use paths for cyclists and walkers edge most of the lakes and ponds and so I

24   Lee Valley Park, https://www.leevalleypark.org.uk.

spotted a little heron through the languid willows, and heard the geese flying in from wintery climes to join friends and be given a noisy welcome on one of the scrapes. Occasionally grassy mown tracks bisected a larger island and I walked through between big willows and overgrown hedges. Here fallen trees were used as playgrounds for children to climb over; or were carved into whatever shape the sculptor fancied. Or just to sit on.

And so, by wander and wonder I reached Waltham Town Lock. Here the pound lock allows for two-way traffic but just along from it is the Lee Valley White Water Centre,[25] a downhill one way only course. Down sweep the canoeists in a turmoil of water, back surges, deep drops, whirlpools, trying to stay not just upright with frenzied paddling but to guide the canoe through the specified course. How to get back up? How to get to the top? How to move canoe and canoeist from the calm gathering pond up to the top of the race? What goes down must go up! They look to be put on an escalator!

I needed something calming after that. A visit to the Waltham Abbey Royal Gunpowder Mills Museum sounded interesting but not what I wanted, so I took the train through to Ely. Quite a change of countryside beyond Cambridge as we entered fenland. Fields of dark peaty soil raised on ramparts above drainage ditches looked like sweetcorn grown in chocolate bars. The well-marked walking route from the station past the marina, through the Jubilee Gardens, and into the parkland of Cherry Hill led me up to the Cathedral.

The Almonry restaurant in the undercroft of the Cathedral appealed for lunch and there I was back into

---

25 Lee Valley White Water Centre, https://en.wikipedia.org/w/ index.php?title=Lee_Valley_White_Water_Centre&ol-did=1039263539 (last visited Dec. 26, 2021)

Covid security again, almost forgotten about in the fresh air and spaciousness of the Lee Valley. In the café I had visited the first evening of this trip I had felt cramped and disturbed by the lack of interest seemingly in 'covid security'. The pub I transferred to thereafter had the NHS Test & Trace paper system at the entrance. I chose a table nearby for better ventilation and fairly near the bar but, as I couldn't always get the food ordering system to work, I then had to approach the bar as best I could along marked pathways. As the sky darkened and the queue lengthened at the door, I saw that a security guard had come on duty to control entry into the pub.

In the Almonry staff shielded in visors wrote down Test and Trace details then led me to a sanitised table seat. The building itself enforced social distancing and table service followed. Likewise, when I entered the Cathedral itself, Test and Trace details were required. But it was worth it. Without seats filling the nave its colourful floor could be seen as a true partner of the painted roof overhead, leading to the most remarkable feature of the Cathedral[26] itself, the octagonal lantern. A small model demonstrated its structure. Everything holds everything together when everything is in place. But how do you achieve that piece by piece 60 feet above ground and paint it too? People who can do that built St Paul's Dome 300 years later as much as people who built cathedral spires built the Shard in due course.

It was time for a last look around my domain ensuite and all, before coming home. All was back to an impersonal state ready for Covid cleansing. I had been nervous about undertaking this trip. I had tried to be

---

26   Ely Cathedral, https://en.wikipedia.org/w/index.php?title=Ely_ Cathedral&oldid=1057770116 (last visited 22 December 2021).

canny about it, to travel outside of anything like a rush hour. To stay with an organisation I knew and trusted in an area where I could spend most of the time out of doors. I had managed and accepted the limitations and looked forward to returning when they had eased. What's the Lee Valley like north of Broxbourne, I wondered? But I had also learned sufficiently of the efforts of the staycation industry to brave further.

About 90 minutes from leaving, the sun shone warmly over the rolling fields and woods of the Weald. And the welcome home sight of the solid north face of the Sussex Downs.

18. Staying Away

10 October 2020

No. of UK cases: 15,166
Since July, I have been reporting my state of Covid health to the King's College/Zoe Covid Symptoms Study,[27] and from October have recorded the number of cases for Worthing as estimated by that study.[28]
Number of estimated Worthing cases: 90

I stopped at the entrance to my staycation hotel to zap the NHS Test and Trace QR code it offered. I was not sure I needed to as they had all the paperwork about me from my booking, but I was quite pleased to think I

---

27 Source for this data and as subsequently Zoe, https://covid. joinzoe.com. Similarly for

28 ©Openstreetmapcontributors; www.openstreetmap.org.

had mastered the trick. The first time after downloading the app, I switched the phone on when I left the house but did not switch on the app itself. It's not that clever, though!

Next time I went to the shop I did switch it on as I approached and, as there was no queue could struggle to align the camera with the code. Finally, the Big Tick came on screen and I looked up triumphant. There was now a long queue. Its leader said coldly, 'Someone's come out – go in.' I rushed in forthwith, then half-way round the shop realised the face mask was still in my hand – not on my face! At the till, I mentioned to the young assistant the difficulty I had had, and he looked surprised. But was this surprise that anyone would bother, or surprise that anyone would find it a problem to zap a large code that was down at knee height?

In the reception area, not only was there a reminder to wear a face mask hereon in but reminders abounded of hands, face, space protection. The receptionist was safe inside the screen but was not interested in the paperwork I offered to prove I was me, nor did she hand over the keys direct. Instead, she passed me an envelope that contained the room keys – sanitised – and directed me to my room. Through several fire doors I passed, each stating a face mask should be worn beyond. I hoped this did not mean that was cumulative! The corridor off which my room led smelt pleasantly, and I realised that it came from a block of air disinfectant/sanitiser.

Throwing my case onto the luggage stand, I headed for the view and the necessary accompaniment, a nice cup of tea. But no nice china to take it in. A brown corrugated cardboard mug stood by the kettle. And no silver spoon to stir with, just a brown cardboard stirrer. All easily disposable stuff. But a good supply of tea, coffee and milk. I took stock of the room. There was no flash across the duvet at the foot of the bed. There was no literature, stationery or other such on the desk. That was no great problem, but, oh dear, there was no hairdryer in any drawer! It was time to read the explanation in the envelope.

In short, now that I had entered the room, no one else would until I vacated it. And so, Reception would provide generous supplies of coffee and milk packs without demur. The rubbish bin looked to be of sufficient size. And I would make my own bed! Self-sufficient staycationing in another form!

The sun was still shining as I sallied forth into the town. I looked for a drop-box for keys at reception but that was covered over. The keys were mine to have and to hold until I departed. Nor was there any literature around, I now realised, about the wonders of the area. In the place of the usual bureau of literature, a desk with sanitisers and wipes had been placed.

It was not an area I had ever visited previously so I spent a happy hour or two wandering around as I spied interesting footpaths that went here, there, or somewhere. Following these up would keep me happy in the next few days. However, this piece isn't about those jolly jaunts nor about the usual reasons for which people choose holiday accommodation and destination. Rather it is to give an idea of the effort the staycation industry is making to keep us secure, and that staying away from home is not impossibly reckless.

I returned to my accommodation, giving myself time for a drink before dinner. Masks were required as I found my way around the passages and common ways to the bar and lounge. The comfortable armchairs were arranged in groups according as the layout of the lounge demanded or provided. But the groups were the regulation two metres apart. I could talk with fellow drinkers in my group but speaking across the divide to another group was quite a challenge.

The bar staff, wearing black face masks, came to us to take and bring orders and take payment by card. But it just seemed discourteous that, while they addressed me from behind a mask, I spoke to them without one. A kind of imbalance that had a note of class distinction to it.

Dinner was served in the Restaurant by face-masked staff, with the usual choices for each course. How then, I wondered, was breakfast to be served when the usual buffet was not to be? Room service? Pre-book? Takeaway? No! A menu detailed the various cold offerings available and described the 'Full English' and the cooked alternatives, to be served with full table service. The waiting staff patiently tried to take note of what variation anybody would want. But breakfast is such a personal meal; not just with or without – black pudding, sausage, baked beans etc., but all the choices one makes for oneself at a buffet, the bacon well-cooked or undercooked; fried eggs sunny side up (or not). Toast came with the breakfast as standard.

So no buffet meant no way to create one's own combination of cereals, mixing crunchers, cracklers, shredded or pressed to one's own satisfaction. No queue of guests waiting to serve themselves from a shared warming pot of porage, and to comment on the qualities of the morning's offering; assuming that was served at the best of times. Nor was there the opportunity to discuss how the toast machine worked, and whether it was over browning or under cooking the bread.

I could now see what was involved in preparing the tables. The table was cleared of all china and a marker placed to show the table as out of use for the time being. As staff became available, they sloshed sanitiser over the top of the table and the sides. Likewise, the chairs were sprayed with sanitiser. Then the marker was replaced to show the table was ready for use.

After a few happy days it was time to depart. The room cleaner knocked on my door to see if I had left. Not quite ready; I was running a bit late. She was wearing a visor and pinny which, as I had read, she was required to change between cleaning each room, and she carried an array of sanitisers, cleaners etc. I had felt safe there. They had thought through the arrangements, and their side of things was well organised. It was then up to me and fellow guests to play our part in keeping us all well and I reckoned we had done a good job. One-way passageways and separate entrance/exits had been marked where possible. I witnessed a male guest coming out against the flow and direction on one occasion and there was a murmur of disapproval by those around!

Home and back to the permanent self-catering. And tea in a china mug.

from 14 October 2020

The Three Tier system is introduced. Most of the country including Worthing is placed in Tier 1 (medium), with restrictions continuing unchanged.

19. Just a Bit Mislaid!

20 October 2020

No. of UK cases: 21,331
No. of estimated Worthing cases: 149

The 'Avocet' trainline begins at Exeter and, having stopped at the pretty little Devon villages of Topsham and Lympstone, heads down the Exe estuary, where these graceful birds, with their distinctive curved beaks, overwinter in the upper reaches. Further down the estuary the geese noisily proclaimed their presence as my train passed by, its wheels almost in the water. I doubt if any rail line is named for them! The single-track line continues to this day right close alongside the Exe estuary, with wide views across the water to the hills beyond, and into Exmouth.

Now the line ends here but years ago you could continue on as the line cut the corner across to Budleigh

Salterton on the seacoast. [29] However, the track from Exmouth to Budleigh Salterton has become part of the National Cycle Path No 2. (shown on OS.115 'Exmouth & Sidmouth'). I picked up the trail in Exmouth on the southern edge of Phear Park.

Like the old steam train, no doubt, I puffed slowly up the half-mile incline. Dogs, their walkers, and a buggy-driver amassed around the exit, but as a practitioner of the new etiquette (as of summer 2020) I dutifully hung well back until their conversation ceased. The negotiation of the busy Saltern Road and Littleham Road was well signed and so I turned into Jarvis Close, a bungalow area. The old track has survived modern developments and now even has a name, Hudsons Way as, in its direct fashion, it passes between fences and gardens. One more road to cross and I was free of the urban world into the countryside.

Just enough curve in the direction to make it interesting, just enough tantalising view of the forward path to keep one going. I enjoyed views over the Devon countryside, its amazing cherry-red soil, its intertwining fields and hedgerows. The path remained true and the tarmac was replaced with gravel. The general trend of the land was downwards though I couldn't see the sea. The trees grew tall but through them the warm sunshine was filtered by the autumn leaves.

The occasional cyclist passed me, some intent, non-speaking, but one or two friendly, hand-waving ones. Then I heard the regular beat of a determined walker coming ever closer. A young woman gave me a brief nod and passed me by, a true speed walker, a London-by-lunchtime lady.

29 Budleigh Salterton Railway, https://en.wikipedia.org/w/index. php?title=Budleigh_Salterton_Railway&oldid=1019798953 (last visited Dec. 22, 2021

I stopped again just to enjoy being out, feeling well, lovely day, lovely scenery, a straight path behind me and empty one ahead. Oh no! There she was appearing, already two bends ahead of me. There are many ways to enjoy walking.

The access to Castle Lane came and went as did a few dogwalkers. The path took a definite downhill tilt, and the surface became increasingly soft and more muddy. It grew darker too, not because the day was clouding over but because the trees, growing out of the side of the deep cutting, had become even taller, the canopy more dense. A road passed high overhead on its solid red Victorian abutments but there was no access to it, nor did I want one. It was so easy to keep walking on and on, and so very pleasant.

But then came a signpost – permissive path to the left with the N2 logo wrapped around it. Yet the tarmac path also continued trending right, surely equally sound. My intention had always been to leave the N2 path at a point of my own determining as it disappeared altogether from the map somewhere in the NW environs of Budleigh Salterton. Was this my chance?

I took the permissive path and followed its grassy track; certainly it was not the rail track. And came to a T-junction. A lane stretched to my right and left. No footpath sign. No N2 logo. Where was I? I began to regret the carefree, if not careless, way I had been merrily walking along, not checking my position on the map. I was not, of course, lost; I never am. But I was, I had to admit, just a bit mislaid!

I checked the instructions I had taken off the internet, which were verbal rather than visual. 'Keep going till you get to the end and then stop' was its advice, though said at great length. But that was my problem. Was this the end – where it fell off the map? It was a moment when I could have done with a comfortable seat and a nice cup of coffee.

Better than that, a friendly and helpful local cyclist came along, and quickly read the OS map. 'Oh yes. Go down here and at the junction, there's a bus stop close by, if you want one.' I followed the lane south and must have passed where the cycle track proper crossed the lane. I reached civilisation, but no bus stop was to be seen. Fortunately, a passer-by could point it out – behind a big white van and under an overhanging tree – and volunteered the time of the next bus.

I stood at the stop and checked my watch – 25 minutes till the bus was due. Pity there wasn't a seat as well, but I had opportunity to open my local town map and work out my position. Of course! All I had to do was walk down the lane opposite, turn right and by the time the bus came there I would be. Which I did very pleasantly and soon was celebrating my arrival on Budleigh Salterton foreshore with a well-filled crab sandwich.

For those who want to make a circular walk, the usual way back to Exmouth is along the Southwest Coastal Path. I had followed that the previous day from Exmouth to Orcombe Point,[30] where the estuary meets the sea, then walked beyond, to the High Land of Orcombe. I had seen the northwards coast upping and downing, inning and outing, and that was enough. Home by bus!

I walked back up the high street, with its small shops set back from narrow pavements, and considered how the new etiquette had evolved since the summer. People are rather more confident, rather less fearful of being out

---

30 National Trust: https://www.nationaltrust.org.uk/exmouth/fea-tures/orcombe.

and about. With more people in the streets, it was not now practical to keep a full social distance of two metres. That had contracted to about one metre at the most but was balanced by an increase in the use of face masks, as the requirement to wear them in shops and buses filtered into wearing them on the streets. It's also easier in some ways to keep them on, perhaps at half-mast, than to try to unstring them from one's ears, where they may have become tangled with spectacles and hearing aids. And now winter approaches, they have their uses to keep the face warm and dry. The standard of the masks has risen too, as more people wear more stylish masks! It's how each of us negotiates our own way of living with Covid long term, balancing the risks as best we each can.

The bus was waiting, appropriately enough, in Station Road, but it was not so named in honour of the bus station but for the old railway station. This was where the cycle path-cum-rail track should properly have arrived! But, apart from a length across the Green, the town map indicated the way would be along suburban roads and through modern town development. The route I had taken was rather better for a walker, and probably half a mile shorter too. The ongoing route of the old railway could also be better traced by a walker as the map showed a not quite continuous line of footpaths that trended east out of the town. These, probably, are on the rail track until it headed northwards up the flatlands of the River Otter. Intriguing!

The bus struggled up West Hill out of Budleigh Salterton, then up Knowle Hill, and I looked down into the deep, tree-lined canyon I had walked a few hours before. It was not an old green lane sunk below road height from all the wear and tear of countless feet and creaking cartwheels. It did not have a natural geological cause. It was not worn down by water and wind but was man-made for the railway project. Awesome!

There is yet another way of returning from Budleigh Salterton to Exmouth, neither along the coast nor on the old rail track but somewhere in between. That's what the map shows anyway. So, come next spring, weather and Covid and everything else permitting, maybe I shall return and try this route. It's nice to have something to look forward to!

Getting Serious

from 5 November 2020

National restrictions are introduced (Lockdown 2) for four weeks.

People can leave home only for specific reasons and can meet one person not of their household or support bubble, outdoors, only.

Non-essential high street businesses, including personal care and hospitality must close but takeaways and deliveries are allowed

20. Bah! Humbug!

11 November 2020

No. of UK cases: 22,950
No. of estimated Worthing cases: 497

On a mild autumn morning, as a wistful sun peered through the clouds, I too was opening the curtains and thinking to go out into the grey world of Lockdown 2. Somehow or other, the habit, the discipline of doing regular local walks had faltered during the summer months. The summer heat, when it happened, had been one good reason. I had done other walks if not the regular walks. There was always the garden growing despite the heat, the rain, the wind – or because of. And this summer I had the challenge of a green garden bin to fill.

For years I had filled the car with black sacks of garden rubbish and taken them to the household waste depot. There was a kind of camaraderie to it; when I had overfilled my sack and could not lift it over the chest-high parapet, kind, tall men would heave the stuff over into the locker for me. The staff too were always very helpful in getting all the brambly, thorny, prickly stuff out the car and away. But just before lockdown proper settled in, in March, I had taken a carload there, not realising that social distancing was now in force. Only half the number of bays were in use. A 'master of ceremonies' was directing each car to the next available bay, regardless of whether it was anywhere near the relevant locker. It had taken me an hour from the moment of arrival to the moment of escape. And so, I booked in for the green bin service. And, of course, to be sure of getting my money's worth I had filled it every week since, sometimes with my neighbour's assistance.

Once more the green bin was outside the house waiting to be emptied, full to the brim, and the refill for next week's was already, so I was free. I would pack my little daysac with the necessaries and remember to take the mobile phone also. Just a few days before Lockdown 2 commenced, I had stepped into a café where Madam Table Monitor (behind her visor) demanded my name and number before taking me to a table of her choice. No need, I could zap the app. But I had forgotten to switch the phone across from my usual handbag.

Maybe I didn't appreciate the likes of Madam Table Monitor and how they protect us. Certainly, that particular café was busy. Some people obviously do take note. I still can't decide whether I prefer people in visors or face masks. When someone wears a visor, I feel I want to rip it off so that I can see their eyes, which show perfectly well through a visor. When someone wears a mask, it's difficult to hear, and that rectangular strip of cloth across the face is so inelegant and uncompromising.

In a group, before Lockdown 2 began, when we were unexpectedly asked to wear masks, the masks that were produced were all of the batwing type in different shades and patterns. So I have gone upmarket myself and bought a batwing-shaped mask, dark blue, but plain. It's quite thick, so people don't easily hear what I'm saying! On the other hand, it's quite warm! And, having got off the bus still wearing it but facing a chill northerly wind, it was comforting to keep it on.

I suppose the interest at the moment is to see how we all adjust to Lockdown 2; that is, have we developed a way of living with Covid, which seems to us OK and which Lockdown 2 is not largely going to alter. I have, thank goodness, not suffered Covid, nor has anyone else that I directly know. Therefore, I have not given it to anyone either (presumably). Therefore, my way of living with it is OK. Therefore, continuing with my way of going around is OK and I shall not get or give Covid. An argument that is not, of course, valid, but equally one has nothing but past experience as a guide into the future.

The main disruption in Lockdown 2 is, obviously, the limit on seeing friends and family, in the flesh, for real. But also, personal self-regard is challenged as providers, like hairdressers, beauty salons and nail bars are unavailable, as well as the nightlife. What we are left with is the serious stuff, what is worthwhile, essential, though who is to define that? Covid is making Puritans of us all, even though we don't have to live such a puritan life as first time around.

In the meanwhile, I must get out. There is a sort of tedium to Lockdown 2, which is debilitating as the weather declines. Because Lockdown 2 is time-limited, it's easy just to wait for it to go away, and then proper life will return. *Oh no it won't. Oh yes it will – sometime!*

21. The Green Way into Worthing

18 November 2020

No. of UK cases: 19,609
No. of estimated Worthing cases: 426

The slope in Pond Lane Rec. must surely give the home side an advantage, I would think, but it seems a popular venue from the cheers and shouts I hear on Sunday mornings – sorry, *used* to hear. The footpath that leads out southwards heads for Longcroft Park but this trends away from today's walk. I turned away and saw the first surprise of the walk, a 'For Sale' notice up at a nearby neighbour's house. Must find out what they're asking! Further along the road, the tree that had been full of red berries a week ago was already half-stripped; somebody has been stocking up for Christmas! Into Westlake Gardens and past a couple of trees so trimmed and manicured into shape they looked like big green mushrooms. But the bowling greens of Tarring Rec had escaped their manicured look as the grass was taking its chance to grow. The huge oak trees, however, were surprisingly full of leaf, golden in the welcome sunshine.

Up at the top of Durrington Hill it was noticeable that the recent gales had stripped all the trees of their leaves, but as the road descended only the upper branches, those above house height, were bare while the lower ones were still leafed and coloured. Here, in the flatlands, they were golden to the top. The children's park was empty, likewise the tennis courts, which had been surprisingly popular during the summer, and so was the netball court. I had never seen netball played here but, pre-lockdown, this was where a group of men used to foregather regularly, with footballs. I never had time to stop to see what happened when the group swung into action but wondered if this was where they played walking football.

Into Twitten Way; when driving hereabouts it's an area where I don't so much get lost as get found – back where I began. Walking here is different: you can make continual progress forward, joined up walking, from one twitten into Haynes Road and on to the next twitten. I found most of the twittens I know when cycling; seeing the 'no cycling sign' was like a red rag to a bull: just had to go and investigate! At the end of Haynes Road is a small allotment, and there was somebody moving around. You can't see easily into the allotments because of big hedges, alive with chattering birds this morning, so I walked on to the little community garden just beyond. It's a small triangular plot about 30ft long and 15ft wide but occupied by raised beds of flourishing strawberry plants and rich red-gold marigolds, among others. A fig tree with a couple of figs still hanging and several other smallish trees. There's also a seat, but I don't know who gets to sit on it as the gate is always padlocked. And a garden shed.

Seeing a tall figure dressed in yellow oilskins, standing so still he must be a statue, reminded me that while 'his' fish and chip shop was closed as I passed, as a takeaway, it would open later. It's only the fish and chip shops where you sit up to table and put your own salt and vinegar on the chips that have a problem, or who have to redesign themselves as takeaways. Before climbing the stairs, known as 'Jacob's Ladder', over the railway I always stop at the foot to note the octagonal pillars/newel posts made by 'H. Young & Co. Engineers Pimlico London' 150 years, and more, ago. We who live in Southern Region should be thankful for its third rail system for carrying electricity. We only have 20 or so steps up and 20 or so steps down, in two flights. Where the power is carried in overhead cables it requires a third flight of 10 steps up and 10 down to get across.

Having walked through a series of developments from the 1930s to the 70s I was now into sturdy Worthing housing, good Victorian red brick, with high triangular peaked fronts and trees flourishing the length of the well-kept road. It leads into Victoria Park, where the sun was shafting shadows of its big trees across the sunny grass and lighting up the ribbons hanging on a 'shaman' tree too! Someone had noticed a smallish tree with many lower branches and had started to bedeck it with colourful ribbons and cards thereon, in honour of the NHS.

At the top of the park is the activity area. Some boxers were, in turn, taking on a sparring partner. And beside them the adults' free-standing activity machines. They're in quite a few parks and open spaces and, while I look at them with interest, I've never understood what you're supposed to do with them, and they're so heavily built they're not appealing. Maybe you should take the small child's creative approach, as displayed in their section just alongside. Why not consider yourself a performance artist not an athlete and not be constrained by stereotypes, i.e. climb up where adults expect you to slide down or push where they think you should pull and lie down on what somebody meant you to stand up? Or maybe it's a modern sculpture park. No coffee van here today; pity.

Not wanting to head for Worthing's West End, I eschewed the little footpath into the wooded mini park of Park Crescent with its Regency terrace of houses, complete with glistening white pediments and pilasters. I walked along the equally pleasing road of artisan terraced housing, no front gardens and almost no pavements. Quite the modern thing, in a way! At the end the pub stood one side of the road and the church the other. Both were, of course, closed and unable to operate their main function at present. Both hoping to celebrate Christmas, but in different ways.

I walked down the underpass, to be met by a sight of cheering colourful graffiti. Or wall-paintings. And the message 'The only way out is through', though easier to read if you lay on your back. But who by? How come?

I walked on and into Homefield Park. What's the difference between a 'Park' and a 'Rec'? This too has activity areas, which here include a skate park. A boy was skateboarding up and down over the north–south route, while a girl on her scooter rode the mostly flat perimeter course. In the good years the circus pays Worthing a visit on the treelined central green of the park. More trees offer shade to those sitting on the hillocks and humps in a triangular corner area. Dog-walkers, cyclists and those happy to sit and watch the world go by, or just in need of a breather, find a place here too.

Into the last Park of the day, though I've always called Beach House Park 'Beach House Gardens'.[31] When does a 'Park' become a 'Garden'? Red flowers and green-leaved

---

31 Adur & Worthing Councils, https://www.adur-worthing.gov.uk/parks/find/worthing/beach-house-park.

geraniums cheered up a dark bed, but on turning the corner the glory of the park was the Tree of Heaven. Its red, orange and gold leaves large and brilliant as the low winter sun shone through the silvery pampas grasses to turn it into nature's shaman tree, outdoing all others. Past the tribute to the pigeon carriers of the War, I reached the Brighton Road and came up to date with Covid and all that.

There had been a few people on the way, usually just where you would prefer not to meet them, on narrow footpaths, but a polite shrug of the shoulders and we passed back-to-back. But this was a main road and there was not all that much traffic about. I didn't come down here at all in Lockdown 1, which shows the change of things, but the traffic was certainly less than it would have been a year ago. But I was also conscious of the wind as I had not been before and, after walking through Denton Gardens, the lumpy heavy swell of the sea with a few white horses made it visible.

At last, a coffee van. A short queue had dutifully formed, something like two metres apart and all getting out their face masks. Face mask, spectacles, hearing aids – some of us need big ears! I watched with amazement the purchase being made ahead of me, the top-of-the-range hot choco, complete with swirls of cream, mini marshmallows, and a crumble of toffee over. My turn, what a comedown: 'small black americano please'. But there was a holiday atmosphere on the Prom. People were walking happily about, enjoying the fellowship of their companion, keeping apart but enjoying the presence of everyone on the sunniest day for days.

It was not so in the town. The mood changed as I left Steyne Gardens and turned into the main shopping area. So many shops were shut because of the rules; so many were shut, period. There is usually a busy market down the length of Montague Street but today just a few stalls, mostly selling bread or vegetables or food generally. There was a tenseness to everyone, tension seen almost in their faces and as they hugged themselves to themselves, wishing everyone else was not there. It is as if having joined together against a common enemy in the spring we are, in the autumn, becoming suspicious of others. We are doing the right thing, we believe, therefore it must be other people who are the cause of the present situation. Or maybe it is a touch of guilt that maybe we shouldn't be there at all.

Maybe, also, it is a tension caused by trying to make a start on making Christmas happen when so many shops are shut, and planning for Christmas so uncertain. I missed, especially, the charity shops and their supply of Christmas cards. I suppose if you select the card by the charity you can buy them online. But if, like me, you buy the card you like and the good cause comes with it, it's more difficult. Yet, in the gloom, as the sun had been overtaken by cloud, the sparkle of Christmas lights was beginning to outline dark, bare branches in the plaza. I had seen one wreath already hanging on a house door as I walked by. In some windows the Christmas tree has already been placed. Other houses have already slung lights over garden bushes or arranged wonderful set pieces over the frontages.

To the final gardens of the day, Liverpool Gardens, with my takeaway soup and roll. It was just too far and too bleak to go on the Pier. But, with no café open, only takeaways, that was the same conclusion others also were making. Usually it's me, one or two others, and a lot of pigeons and seagulls. Today there were no birds at all, but quite a few people spread along the bench that followed the curves of the Garden. Fortunately, dividers marked out 4ft spaces, not intending that we should sit one space apart but in effect people were doing at least that. But my reason for braving the big city was at hand.

As the clock struck the hour, I moved on, homeward bound via the dentist. I had had the boiler serviced. The car had passed its MOT. Now it was the turn of my teeth. Regular events mean that as soon as one is done, the next looms up, in six or so months' time. But in Covid times a cheerful 'See you then', opens up a prospect of uncertainty.

from 2 December 2020

The Four Tier system is introduced.

Most of the country is placed in Tier 2 or 3. Worthing is placed in Tier 2 (high alert).

Different households can meet, in groups up to 6, outdoors only.

Pubs and restaurants can open to serve alcohol only with substantial meals, only by table service, and must close at 11pm.

22. 'Tis the Season to Be Jolly

12 December 2020

No. of UK cases: 21,502
No. of estimated Worthing cases: 250

Christmas colour greeted me even as I left the house! The fencing around this week's roadworks were green with red and white markings! And so much colour! Men in green trousers and orange jackets were putting in purple cables. Further on, men in yellow high-vis jackets were placing yellow walkways over channels holding yellow pipes. There's colour-coding for you! I was seeing these through my steamed-up glasses caused by my non-breathable but so far effective face mask. But, by travelling on the bus, I was spared the functional problems of negotiating through narrow traffic lanes, and the nerve-wracking business of manoeuvring from the wrong lane into the right lane to get by.

Time was short. I had been held up by printer problems but after an hour's tense activity, thankfully, it came back to life. But to miss an hour's sunshine on a short December day is to lose precious moments. I had been feeling bunkered in the last few days of grey dreary wet, cold windy weather and the resolve required for Tier 2 was fracturing but, at the same time, it was an effort to go out and brave the public world.

I wanted to make arrangements to meet friends and, in accordance with Tier 2 rules, these meetups must be outside. We are now allowed family socialising in the Christmas relaxation, but so much of Christmas is about the wider family, our family of friends, and there is no let up for that.

The purpose of my outing was to check out the delightful Marine Gardens[32] on West Worthing seafront as a suitable outside venue where our group of High Salvington Windmill volunteers could meet. It had been our custom to host in the confines of our workspace a 'Christmas office party', whereby to celebrate our friendship and common interests. Not this year. It was some relief to find that not only the bowling pavilion, which guarded the green emptiness before it, offered shelter, but also the water garden at its side offered plenty

---

32 Adur-Worthing Councils, https://www.adur-worthing.gov.uk/
     parks/find/worthing/marine-gardens.

of seats and protection from whichever way the winter wind was blowing (I hope), and the café was a source of provision. But a bit cheerless all the same.

It's not the year for office parties, club dinners, group socials. There could be no association coffee mornings or fellowship lunches. In place of celebrating years of friendship among the filing cabinets or in a comfy warm pub, fires lit, Christmas trees and lights around, the clink of glasses, the sound of happy cheerful voices, the bursts of laughter and even singing, this year we must meet in the park, or along the seafront, shielding from the December wind and weather as best we can. Each to bring their own fish and chips or other takeaway packed in a polystyrene box. Horrible stuff in horrible colours. Soapy feel. But it probably does keep the food warmer than newspapers, and less handling and wrapping is required.

Nor will there be the usual 'Carols around the Fire' at the Mill, held the Friday before Christmas with a collection for a local good cause. Indeed, organising even a collection is fraught with problems. No Carol Concerts in churches or public halls. No *Messiah* being sung by any of the music societies of the area. No Salvation Army brass band oompahing its warm and cheerful way through traditional carols and equally traditional non-carols. However, numbers of Covid cases in Worthing are down considerably on what they were a month ago, according to the survey I follow (see footnotes 27 & 28).

Duty done, decision made, I joined the cheerful crowds along the Prom, in the clear winter sunshine. We were all walking quickly just to keep warm but there was still plenty of space for social distancing. Wonderful hats came out from the back of the cupboard, colourful woolly ones in this weather. Volunteers clearing the hedges of gardens wore red 'elves' bonnets, though no reindeer antlers were yet to be seen. Christmas is still a couple of weeks away. A few toughies were devoid of headgear altogether. But friendly, relaxed warmth exuded from all to all. Much of Christmas is about the run up. The great day comes and is meant to be the sum and purpose of it all, but sometimes it is better to travel hopefully than to arrive.

Children moved around in their seaside playground, practising Robinson Crusoe living, playing with sand, climbing wooden structures, finding the upright wood-carved shark-cum-noticeboard a little daunting, swinging in the makeshift seating. The metre-square rocks planted and spaced out among the shingle of the beach as sea defences, each weighing a ton or more, were lit by the low sun. The 'keep off – danger' signs were an obvious invitation to do just that. Where did they come from? How? Silhouetted figures against the sharp light were taking their opportunity to walk the long beach.

I took my cappuccino at the coffee van and paid by card. It's surprising how even the smallest establishment now accepts cards without demur by some wonder trick of combining mobile phone and calculator. Indeed, it is preferred against the perils of handling cash, and 'contactless' has become a noun in its own right.

I joined the adults wandering on, looking at the Waterwise Garden[33] along the Prom. Here, in this extreme environment of salt-laden air, shingle and strong winds, a garden of drought tolerant plants has been created. I always think of it as 'the wooden garden' as it includes driftwood sculpture, planked paths and rough benches among the shingle, and a walkway out towards the sea.

---

33   https://www.adur-worthing.gov.uk/parks/find/worthing/
     waterwise-garden/

The great thing about this incursion into desert island living is that you can go home for a shower and tea afterwards! But one last experience to enjoy, and a reminder we do live on an island, if not desert. The sunset! We in the south have the good fortune to see in winter the sun set below the horizon. The best spectacle of the day was, as so often, provided by nature as a hugely scarlet red round sun was caught between dark clouds above and a darkening sea beneath waiting, ready to enfold and save it for another day.

Anyone who has created their own calendar with times of sunrise and sunrise, as I have for the last few years, will have noticed that the sun has a double life as regards heading north. The afternoon sun takes, in mid-December, a very brief stand and then heads north. Sunset on Sunday 20 December is back as it was on 5 December, about 10 minutes before 4pm and, around January 1, sunset is past the hour. Hurrah! But the morning sun still stays on the move south until it takes its Twixmas rest: say, 0805 on Christmas Day to 0805 on New Year's Day. Even so, it doesn't like getting up on dark mornings any more than the rest of us, so it is not till the middle of January that sunrise occurs the right side of 8am.

Although the young were still playing on the waterwise playground, and adults still stood in the 'wooden garden', the queue for the coffee van had shortened, cars were pulling out from the unwanted, unused coach spaces. The walkers were becoming ever more shadowy and merging into the twilight. The Christmas lights were coming on in the houses. It was time to get home and set up my own modest arrangement in the window. From there, I can look out to the end of the sun's southerly run and for the day when its return and the new year of promise begins.

We can all look to summer now in hope with the arrival of the first vaccine and the first people jabbed.

> *Ring out the old, ring in the new*
> *Ring happy bells across the snow.*
> *The year is going, let him go.*
> *Ring out the false, ring in the true.*
>
> *Ring out old shapes of foul disease.*

Tennyson, *In Memoriam*[34]

34 *In Memoriam* https://www.public-domain-poetry.com/al-fred-lord-tennyson/ring-out-wild-bells-755

23. Food Forethought

22 December 2020

No. of UK cases: 36,804
No. of estimated Worthing cases: 301

The problem I had given myself was that, having chosen to Collect the main event of Christmas Dinner, a guinea fowl, from a supermarket on the east side of Worthing, how to get there?

The most efficient way is along the A27, built on the foothills of the Downs, so slight ups and downs, but basically going in the right direction. It is an old road which served well as a bypass while Worthing remained a coastal village. Only since the town jumped it in the last 100 years has there been a problem. Walking beside the

A27 might have been possible in the time of lockdown, but with traffic closely back to normal – old normal, that is – that is not a welcome idea. An alternative would be to walk along Poulters Lane, the old Littlehampton to Broadwater Road. It is now a busy bus route, again not ideal for a walker. But whichever road you take eastwards from Durrington you finish up with the problem of getting round Broadwater Green, still upholding its tradition of cricket on the green in summer. Take the north way and you are back on the A27; go south and you're losing ground as you have to return north again.

In any case, other things need to be considered. Having decided when lockdown began, so long ago, to do my own shopping, I needed to play it canny. That meant, in the first instance, to decide on the size and type of shop to go to. I worked on the Goldilocks principle of not too big, not too little, but just right. In the hectic period just before lockdown, I had (as already mentioned) been unable to buy eggs and had, in my desperation, gone into any shop I came across. But the experience of squeezing around the alleyways, or between the cupboards and fittings of small stores and, as I tried to leave from one, getting involved with someone else coming in, decided me that that size shop was too small.

On the other hand, in the big supermarkets there just seemed too many people around, on too many random journeys. In due course, the supermarkets became better organised with arrows on the floor to encourage shoppers to move sequentially through the store. And introduced the early-morning shopping hour or so, primarily for NHS workers and the elderly. I eschewed even this, partly because I don't like getting up early. It seemed to me that it brought together the very folk who were the more likely to be potential Covid carriers or sufferers.

I did do this once as I needed some lawn seed so was grateful that the supermarket's omnivorous appetite for stock included this. I arrived at about 0745 to see the queue well established in the designated area of the car park. I dutifully followed the guide markings and walked up and down the files to take my place umpteenth from the entrance. The doors opened and the first tranche was waved in. We went on waiting and a few at a time followed in. Finally, I too was in the shop, and in the foyer area bought my lawn seed and walked out again. There was no queue. There was no one waiting to go in. Why did I bother?

Friends who were shielding or such were extremely grateful for the supermarket services of delivery and the priority that was given to them, but it did not suit my style of shopping and I could not get myself sufficiently disciplined to do that. I just like getting this from here, and that from there. And I expanded my knowledge of the range of goods online.

I would stick with the middle-size shop. Fortunately, there were three quite close, even if the available choice was a bit limited and a bit expensive. By the time the lockdown rules eased and the rule of staying at home was relaxed, I had become a little weary of the basic but helpful choice available in my selected shops. My solution was to look at the footfall graphs available online and to decide that the late morning was a good option. The shops too had by this time a better grip on security and had found a way to put screens around their cashiers at the till.

But it was still difficult for shop staff. I had waited outside in the queue at one operating the 'one in one out' arrangement, and as I judged fit had entered the shop. But the doorkeeper had promptly shooed me out. I was a bit miffed as I was replacing only the one who had left. But she said rather abruptly that there were too many people in 'her' shop, so I returned to the queue self-conscious, feeling embarrassed. But then I realised how tired the doorkeeper was, how nervy if not frightened, how uncomfortable she was in that role.

I have seen a shop assistant in tears. It was before Lockdown. I was waiting for the couple at the till to move on. They seemed to be a bit intense and the assistant was standing against the back wall, possibly. They walked out and I moved to the till, whereupon the assistant burst into tears, muttered 'sorry;' and rushed for the back room. I expected another staff member to come, but a few minutes later, she returned, red eyed and downcast and we completed the transaction in silence. Not nice.

So, I patronised my favourite shops accordingly. Indeed, it was quite remarkable to be able to park easily, near to the entrance and feel unthreatened by the overclose presence of other shoppers. The natural sense of private space we have and need at all times was easily extended by the requirements of social distancing and, on the whole available. But as we all became more at ease with the Covid situation, so the numbers of shoppers and their cars returned to something like 'old' normal. And, later, wearing masks in shops became mandatory.

Now, at Christmas, I did want to do the Big Shop at the Big Shop. But I did not want to get involved in the hassle of shopping inside the shop itself – back to my original problem with such establishments. The conclusion was to go for the click and collect arrangement and choose such items as would make it worthwhile and cost effective. Given the amount of stuff I would buy, and the dreariness of the walk, I would take the car. This would also give the car an outing, having had so little use this year.

In any case, a year ago, when I had walked over to this supermarket, I had been rewarded with the Big Breakfast at the neighbouring pub. That was not now possible. Then, after the Big Breakfast and at the appointed hour, I had seen a small notice in the outskirts of the car park indicating the click and collect venue and approached a solitary van complete with bored driver. He took my order number, retired to the chill compartment of the van, produced Christmas Dinner, and returned to his lonely cab.

This year, so different. At first no sign of the click and collect stop until I realised it was now big business and had taken over a complete section of the car park. I joined the queue – so it must be Christmas – and gave my name to the attendant, who then directed me to one of 10 bays to park the car. In due course, another attendant came out from the store pushing a trolley laden with crates. And delivered mine for me to transfer the goodies into the boot of the car. Unfortunately, the goodies provided did not include Christmas Dinner itself! But then the attendant went into the shop and was able to take a guinea fowl off the shelves. Thus my overall intention of not going into the shop was fulfilled, but not in the manner expected.

I then drove down to my other supermarket of choice, to buy the rest of Christmas Dinner. One of the reasons I like shopping there is that there is no radio, no jingling bells, no souped-up carols; nothing disturbs the air of concentration as lists are studied, alternatives pondered, decisions taken about preferences; the sudden swoop at an unexpected opportunity; the deep sigh at the sight of an empty rack where what was once was no more; the puzzled look as the space for some basic item – granulated sugar, let us say – was now given over to an all-butter, all-luxury delightful, delicious, delovely dessert. I, too, had written a list, but left it in the car.

I stood in the queue for the till and pondered the availability and use of self-service machines. In some shops, payment is predominantly by self-service machines, of one kind or another, and few customers go to an assistant. In other shops the machines stand there but largely unused, while the queue for the assistant at the till grows ever longer. In some places too, there are no self -service machines at all, and one has to play the game of guessing which queue is the quicker, which is the till next likely to cease just as one closes in on the end game, and which is the till next likely to open and is one well-placed to jump across thereto.

Stopping on the way to deliver the last couple of Christmas cards – job done, what a relief – I was home for Christmas, and the sort of 'we've made it' feeling of satisfaction that brings. With the food safely stowed away, the Christmas tree decorated with gold-foil wrapped 'presents' (as purchased), and the candles lit (switched on), it was time to rest and relax, to enjoy, and to be thankful.

> *Some hae meat and canna eat,*
> *And some wad eat that want it,*
> *But we hae meat and we can eat,*
> *Sae let the Lord be Thankit!*

Robert Burns, 'The Selkirk Grace'[35]

---

35   The Selkirk Grace, https://sco.wikipedia.org/w/index.php?title=The_Selkirk_Grace&oldid=844978 (last visited 26 December 2021).

Back Inside

from 26 December 2020

Worthing is moved into Tier 4, essentially local lockdown.

People may not leave home without a 'reasonable excuse' but can meet one other person only in public outdoor spaces.

Non-essential retail must close but click and collect is allowed.

Hospitality can operate only via takeaway or delivery.

24. The Long Haul

4 January 2021

No. of UK cases: 58,784
No. of estimated Worthing cases: 1,183

*B*oth *wheelie bins! That's a surprise*, I had thought I was doing well just to work out the day the bin needed to be put out, after four Sundays in a row for Christmas, then three indeterminate days, then another three Sundays for the New Year. The day had been confirmed as I heard the sound of a neighbour's bin being trundled out: a sound that has on occasions roused me from slumber or at least inertia to get my bin out before the bin men arrive. And today would be – should be – the blue-top recycling bin. But, as I put that outside the gate, I saw the neighbours had that out *and* the black-top refuse bin as well. But that never happens!

For several years now, Worthing Council has collected the blue-top (recycling) and the black-top (refuse) wheelie bins on alternate weeks, and the green garden bin every week. Then, come the Bank Holidays, the collection day moves on an appropriate number. And so, consulting my calendar, on which I dutifully mark the colour of the bin in the appropriate-coloured ink on the appropriate day, and carefully transferring the pattern from the old to the new calendar, I had determined that today was blue-top day! But the neighbours had put out both bins. And the neighbours are always right.

I retired in search of the checklist the council had sent some months back, valid until next September. Indeed so! Unlike last Christmas, both bins were to be collected today, but the green garden bin would not be collected. Which was a pity as I had spent an afternoon, choosing my weather, to do some editing of my overgrowing shrubs or underperforming bushes. Not only was it to be regretted for that reason but it would have been a rare time when all three bins were out and, therefore, a chance to assess whether this was the moment to rise to a particular challenge!

Many years ago, I had enjoyed a short photography course. It was so long ago, indeed, that only one of the group had a digital camera! It was the first anyone else had ever seen as they then cost, I believe, in the region of £3,000! The rest of us were using film-and-print cameras; so we were interested in the newcomer but underwhelmed by it. It probably had a resolution and capacity well below that of today's cheapest digi camera.

The cold but bright morning was just the weather for a day's photoshoot on location. The task was to take a photo of three items, but the tutor was keen to emphasise *photo* as much as *three*. He had given that instruction to a previous group and had then been shown by a student a photo of three wheeliebins, in the belief that would suffice. I can't remember how I satisfied the brief but came away from the course feeling challenged. Is it possible to make a *photo* of *three* wheelie bins? They are, surely, as unphotogenic as anything could be. Ungainly, awkward proportions, wider at the top than the bottom, flat drab colours, rounded corners.

They are, indeed, a product of hard-working industrial design and thought, to do the job, to be pulled here and there, contain just about anything and, in the end, to be upturned and emptied with a spine-breaking thunk into the bowels of the waste truck. In short, they are not designed for a static photo. They are designed to be on the move. Nor do they glide around in an upright posture like Daleks but travel at a jaunty angle with a characteristic gritty sound. To do them justice they need a movie, a video, even a choreography! Anyone want to make a video of them moving about and around, each with their speedwalking escorts, lids opening and shutting, lifted high onto the truck, deposed therefrom and returned? Dance of the Binz? Waltz of the Wheelies? But it is better that the bins do the athletics than, as of old, the dustmen did, heaving and twisting steel dustbins onto their backs and into the dustcart.

The fortnightly collection of the recycling blue bin is in itself useful, as it gives yet more time to have a last desperate search for items that have gone AWOL, like teaspoons. I did find the lid of the teapot there one time! It provides a second chance to cut out from the magazine the interesting item you meant to read, but somehow never did until it was too late – almost. Somehow, though, the missing item always gets to the bottom. Whatever it is, is always just out of reach and at that point you realise how deep wheelie bins are. You have to be very tall or have very long arms to have a good turnover of all the papers, bottles, tin and plastic castoffs. Anything from pliers, serving tongs or proper pick-up tools come to the rescue. Of course, that makes all the glass chink, and the tins clank, and the papers rustle to the annoyance of the neighbours.

Bin day has become a marker of the week and possibly the day we meet the neighbours, or at least hear them. Especially the late-night trundler! But also the day the wheelie bin men come, or rather its change, marks the seasons and time of the encircling year. Particularly so at present when so many of the temporal landmarks are lost in the fog and uniformity of Covid.

Bank Holidays in lockdown were marked only by the confusion over when was bin day. Easter and spring brought the double change in date for Good Friday and Easter Monday. Then the mayhem of May, as the holiday on the first Monday, May Day, was duly followed by the Spring Holiday of the last Monday, formerly Whitsun. And last spring that was compounded by VE Day. At one stage in May I thought we had already had wheelie bin day for the week, but in discussion with my neighbour at the Thursday Clapping – remember those? – we agreed wheelie bin day was the following Monday. We were both wrong. It became Friday because of VE Day.

Then the long haul across the arc of summer unmarked this last year by the Olympics, or football finals or even Wimbledon. It was more marked by what we did not do. We did not go away then. We did not visit there. We did not see them. The Last Night of the Proms, a celebration of the passing of the summer and turn of the year did occur, sort of, a fortnight or so after the late August Bank Holiday and the Last Change of Bin Day.

So, wheelie bin day is back to where it began the year. Whichever day starts the year of the wheelie bin is its day throughout the downhill run of autumn until the complex pattern of Christmas and the New Year reset it. Will we have better things than changing bin days to mark our calendars in 2021? Vaccine jab day, as the gateway to normality, at least, let's hope.

And, although we have days for this and that, all marked by change in wheelie bin days, we never have a day in honour of wheelie bins themselves, and the tough, cheerful and friendly crew who come by our gates every week through the heat of summer and the chill of winter to empty and return the bins to the house. For wheelie bins also mark our own temporality as, while we may move on, they stay with the house

25. Hibernia UK

12 January 2021

No. of UK cases: 45,533
No. of estimated Worthing cases: 2,093

Hibernia is the name the Romans gave to Ireland, from a Greek rendering of the Celtic name.[36] But it is no great verbal switch to use it to describe the UK's current state. They, the powers that be, would, I'm sure, like us all really to *hibernate* till spring comes. I would be quite happy to do that but, although I ate well over Christmas and the scales groan whenever I go anywhere near them, I am not up to it. Nevertheless, in Lockdown 3 we are back to the basic

---

36 Hibernia, https://en.wikipedia.org/w/index.php?title=Hibernia&oldid=1054033918 (last visited 22 December 2021).

command: stay at home, look out the window, watch nothing and nobody go by, again. Life is on hold even though it is not true hibernating. It isn't quite happening: more people and cars are going by than in Lockdown 1, I reckon, but maybe not so many as in Lockdown 2.

But it is a cold, clear, sunny winter's day! The frost-laden grass glitters in the warming sun. The roofs opposite are red again after their ghostly appearance in the morning's chill fog. I put on more layers than ever and headed out to take the bus to Worthing seafront. On a recent exercise walkabout, I had seen several buses lingering at their stop to keep to the timetable, which had not been modified for the lack of passengers. And, having counted one passenger shared among the six buses, one being a double-decker, I thought the driver might be glad of my company. So, when I found four other people already on board my bus, it felt quite crowded; all wearing masks, as one now takes for granted.

On the seafront, no one, of course, was doing such but it's a wide pavement, the sun was out, the air was chill, we were all walking quickly, in pairs, in small family groups, as singles. But no coffee van. It must be quite a chilling occupation, not moving much, hands and arms pressing knobs, picking up cups, holding out the pay machine etc., or maybe it was thought too risky as people gathered around. I went to a café reinvented as a takeaway, for sustenance, and was home again, just in time for the daily incantation of Covid numbers. Up again. Seriously. And a friend has reported that she had to self-isolate when family members showed symptoms. I felt guilty about my little outing and also that, perhaps, it may have been risky.

The following day was, however, just as sunny, just as cold. It shows up who has a well-insulated roof and who not – who has a white roof and who the natural colour; black traditional Welsh slate or the occasional shiny Belgian variety, the sea-green pantile roof of 1930s bungalows, the 1950s browny-red tiles, late-20th-century brutalist concrete slabs, or the possibly even heavier, very rare, very old 'Horsham Stone'.[37]

It was too enticing not to go out and we have to take advantage of what sun there is in winter. In short, you feel better for going out in the sun. So that is what I did and why I did it but having left it a little late in the afternoon, the sunlight was difficult to find. It was still flooding my small local park, but I didn't want to walk around and around. I headed for another park, close by. It also has fewer trees, but how to get there by the sunniest route was the problem. It was surprisingly difficult, I kept getting misled by seeing sunlight on the front of a house, but, when I reached that road, I found that at pavement level there was little sun, or, if there was some to start with, the road bent around and I was in the shade and the chill once more.

In narrow twittens it was different. I might just manage to stretch my head into the sun but my feet were still plodding through heavy frost, so much so that when I did have a conversation my interlocutor had been convinced there had been a light fall of snow. I found that some of the customs of Lockdown 1 had returned, people on the path were standing aside once more and were acknowledging the courtesy again. Also, they were ready to enter into conversation reasonably socially distant. Or was that the benefit of enjoying sunshine? In other ways, though, the situation is more relaxed. The shops are not so bothered about numbers of customers.

Yet it now seems a long time since the sad moment just

---

37   Horsham Stone, https://en.wikipedia.org/w/index.php?title=Horsham_Stone&oldid=1028203862 (last visited 22 December 2021).

after the autumn equinox, when the sun's rays cast a light on the wall in my dayroom for the last time. Every winter we need something to look forward to. Something exciting. Like a vaccine jab? I haven't yet had any communication from Them about mine, so I looked at the surgery's website re vaccination, and found a link to an NHS site. At first it seemed to think Worthing was in Scotland! But with its geography corrected it passed me to a booking website, and I stood ready with my NHS number to hand. That was as far as I got. The system soon twigged that I was not yet worthy of the process. Even so, it is not all that exciting a prospect, or perhaps I should take it as a compliment.

If you are able to look out the window and see a garden you can already see spring arriving, slowly but definitely: buds on the lilac, green shoots foretelling crocuses in the lawn, daffodils in the borders, bluebells everywhere, and the rich perfume of hyacinths along the path. Primroses are in flower already, but they are not a great sign of spring for me as, where they are planted on the north side of the house, they are in flower almost the year round. Summer is when they are not, two days running. But some day, lockdown will end, because...

It matters not how far you go
His scaly friend replied,
'There is another shore you know
upon the other side'.

Lewis Carroll, 'The Lobster Quadrille'[38]
Alice's Adventures in Wonderland:

---

38 'Lobster Quadrille', https://www.public-domain-poetry.com/lew-is-carroll.

But what are the quarantine rules there? Will the travel corridor still be open when we want to return? What about self-isolation this end? Is a Covid test required, before or after? Travel brochures promising glorious days of freedom in a golden sunlit landscape thump through our letterboxes this time of year and are gladly received, even more so in this one. But...

And so, I shall book a holiday, for June – in the UK. Have been abroad. Done that. If I want to hear a foreign language spoken of which I do not understand a word, I can go to Wales. It amazes me how different Welsh and Gaelic are from English, yet technically are still part of the same family of languages. And, if you want to see something you haven't seen before, there's plenty of that in Britain. The problem, indeed, is to decide whether to go back to where I went last year and to see and do all the things I didn't quite manage then or, go to a new area. Or do both. They'll be plenty of time, sometime.

But I'll just read the small print in the insurance about Covid, first, before I book.

26. Jab Job Done!

22 January 2021

No. of UK cases: 40,261
No. of estimated Worthing cases: 1,549

As ever, I hesitated when I saw a personal number on the caller display. What kind of scam is this going to be? But, ready with my technique for dealing with such, I picked up the phone. A friendly female voice asked for me by name, which those mis-selling PPI, or telling me my Amazon or my PayPal or some other account I don't have was stopped, do not do. The friendly voice went on to offer me my vaccine jab and seemed as delighted that I accepted on the instant as I was to have the offer! I was amazed how relieved I was to have the call; relieved, but also thankful for all the able people who have made it happen.

I knew other friends who, I thought, were younger than I who had had the jab but were with other surgeries. Had mine, whose premises I have not entered in years, thanks be, overlooked me? One friend already jabbed certainly had health problems, but then another, though older than me and with health problems, had not yet received the call. Relief turned to excitement as I duly left the house the following day, as if to receive a belated Christmas present from Father Christmas himself!

It was not to be at my own surgery but at another, which was on a main road where roadworks were taking place so, unsure of where the car park and especially its entrance was, or how much space there was, I parked nearby. This also enabled me to judge my arrival time better as I had been instructed to arrive not more than five minutes beforehand in order to minimise the queue. As I walked towards the entrance I saw a queue, so promptly joined it. There were two to three people ahead of me, standing socially distant, which gave me time to look around and read the notices, especially the one saying, 'Coronavirus vaccination clinic around the back', with a big arrow!

A young man with a high-vis jacket led me around the building to join another queue of three to four people, and another marshal. As I approached the safe haven of a warm, lighted entrance, the movement of the queue stopped. From the interior stepped another, a monitor rather than a marshal, clipboard in hand. She explained that there was a slight delay as the new shift of four vaccinators was taking place and a new batch of vaccine was being mixed. It would be the Pfizer vaccine and on a noticeboard were its details, the only one of which I understood was the 'best before date' of April. At last, I could leave the outdoor marshals in the cold and the dark and now the rain. I stepped inside with face mask duly in place, to give my name, date of birth, postcode, and state of general well-being for the last fortnight or so, to the clipboard monitor.

A kind gentleman offered me his seat, which I gladly accepted, while the clipboard monitor assured everyone that the order would be as we entered and not where we were seated. As we were in the entrance corridor, we could hear the responses of the newcomers and I had the impression I was about 10 years older than anyone else, until someone turned up seven years older than me. Everyone else also heard her date of birth, with some surprise.

Then someone turned up who had had Covid but was a bit hazy about when this was. Our clipboard monitor went in search of Top Doc, who confirmed that if this was within the last four weeks the lady was not eligible for the vaccine. Our group discussed how it could happen that she had come at all, and it was suggested that if the invite came by text, it was not clear that such a one would not be welcome. It was impressive the effort some people were making to receive the vaccine: being pushed in a wheelchair, leaning heavily on another's arm, or walking independently but with support from a crutch.

So, sitting warm and comfortably, I could now compare this with my expectations. Back in November I had signed up with NHS research and, to my surprise, had been promptly contacted by them and asked to do a Zoom interview the following day. This was my most successful encounter with Zoom as, with any other encounter since with Zoom, something has gone wrong, or at best not really right! However, the matter of my NHS Zoom interview concerned the arrangements for getting the vaccine jab.

I suggested that if they were concerned about OAPs getting the jab their appointment should not be before 1000. My young interviewer asked why, and I explained to her that the free bus pass does not start before 0930! Enlightened, she duly made a note of this, and I was delighted to see on a recent bus trip that West Sussex County Council have rescinded the rules about the use of the bus pass so that OAPs can travel to vaccine appointments freely at any time. I'm sure others made the same point.

I also took my chance to point out that if some identity vetting were needed, the usual is a car driver's licence or current passport, but there are those who do not have either. Overall, I was reassured that the NHS was thinking about and working out in detail the actual delivery of the vaccine.

Now the moment came when I would receive the jab. I followed yet another marshal to the large room. I was shown to my station, where two waited for me, one the vaccinator herself in plastic pinny and face mask, and another seated at a computer behind a screen. I confirmed to her my name and full address. No NHS number, no identity verification required. The vaccinator then went through her drill about health, flu vaccine and Covid symptoms. I admitted to a slight runny nose but assured her this was the usual cold, definitely not Covid. Almost there! Like most people in the room, I was wearing heavy winter coat and woollies, and the problem in winter is to find a bare upper arm. But, having divested myself of my layers, the vaccine was administered very efficiently without pain of any kind.

I was jabbed! I was given a card with the name, date and batch number of this dose, but the card also had space for the date of the second dose. Could this become a kind of 'Covid passport'? I was also given a leaflet explaining the vaccination process. Finally, a label was stuck to my cardigan with my name on and the time I could leave, which would allow opportunity for any reaction to occur.

I was then led to another room, where about a dozen chairs were set out around the walls with a few in the middle set on marks, all duly socially distant, all of us having to do our 15-minute time. It was an odd silence, not the quiet peaceful silence of a meditation group nor the excited eagerness of a group ready for action. We were not really a group at all, just a few people sitting there in a slightly uneasy impatient way waiting for the clock to move. Yet, when people did leave, they did want to acknowledge the shared situation. Some said 'goodbye', others muttered 'best of luck'. All thanked the final volunteer of the day, who escorted us to the exit and sanitised the chairs after they were vacated.

Out in the cold rainy night, at least it wasn't snowing, I avoided the newbies and the queue marshals, and quickly into the car. At home, I noted the Covid numbers of the day, including, especially now, the numbers of vaccinations to have taken place. I was the five millionth person to have the vaccine! Give or take! Or so! Not only did I feel mightily relieved that my own personal situation was now improved and safer, but I also felt surprisingly proud. I do not claim to have saved the nation, or the world, but in my own little way I had done something for the general good.

27. In the Fog

29 January 2021

No. of UK cases: 29,079
No. of estimated Worthing cases: 1,212

*C*an that be a coal fire I smell on the fog-wrapped air? I had walked away from the A27, where passing mega-trucks had slapped my face with their cold, wet, smelly tailwinds. Each had been followed by its retinue of small vans, cars and trucks. Now I stood among the last generation of houses and homes to be built with chimneys, but, even so, was someone actually using a coal fire?

For anyone brought up in a house warmed by coal fires, the smell of coal brings a whiff of nostalgia, for the smoky flavour of bread toasted over the fire; for being able to see deep into red glowing caverns among the embers, ever shapeshifting. When I visited Beamish Living Museum[39] near Durham, I had picked up a lump of coal and brought it away as a souvenir. Beamish has been developed over an actual coal mine and recreates the life and times of a Victorian/Edwardian pit village, overlooked by the steam-powered winding engines.

And there I went into the Co-op shop selling huge bars of Sunlight soap for the washing, and the mangle on sale

---

39   Beamish Living Museum, https://www.beamish.org.uk.

to wring out the surplus water, then entered one of the six miners' cottages and saw heavy cotton sheets hanging up to dry by the coal-fired range – the only source of heat and cooking. The tap was in the yard behind, the communal bread oven at the back of the cottages. I did not have time to go down the coal mine but going underground at other mines has given some appreciation of that tough life, and life above ground was hard too.

But the combination of fog and coal brought back one particular memory. In 1962 I was working in London and my job took me out and about and, in the first week of December into the 1962 London Smog.[40] I can still remember the terror of seeing only a small bubble of evil yellow light ahead and around me that I could not get out of, and yet carried me along with it. I was trapped in a small globe of dim visibility in which shadowy people occasionally appeared in hazy form, from which quickly they disappeared. A kind of social distancing but more like self-isolating.

Not only was space meaningless so too was time. The thick fog, heavy with pollution, and aptly called a 'pea-souper', burned the back of my throat with an acrid taste. I hurried through the silence of the streets, making scary crossings of the roads. By the time I reached the station to take the train home I was breathing fast; my heart was into overdrive. After this claustrophobic day it was so liberating to be in warmth and light and to see defined shapes and real people.

Worthing probably never suffered a smog like that and today, although the fog was dense and low, visibility

---

40   1962 London smog, https://en.wikipedia.org/w/index.php?ti-tle=1962_London_smog&oldid=1053979419 (last visited 22 December 2021).

limited, I was locked into my own world only by fog; there was no smell. I looked along the silent street, each house wrapped in its own thoughts, to see whether any chimney was belching out smoke. In the mild air, a few plumes of steam from central heating units could be seen. The capped chimneys were being used by pigeons as seating. Two sat so still I was surprised when they turned their heads. The smell of coal that started these reflections and memories must have been some kind of aberration. This weekend is the year's mind of the first Covid patients in the UK but, I was thinking, the best inducement to keep lockdown is to have dreary damp weather, without the smog.

I walked on past the school where a few children were being met by their mothers and the little ones were taking their chance to jump, in their colourful wellies, into dark puddles. Snowdrops showed up clean and white against the dark grey headstones in the churchyard. But I still looked along the roofline of the modern houses for a chimney and was unsettled by its absence. Apart from taking the smoke and warmth of the fire upwards, chimneys bring down a lot of fresh air into a room. So, I wondered, too, about the ventilation of modern houses, especially in these Covid times when good ventilation helps to keep the virus at bay.

Continuing my passage, coloured lights, which would have been insignificant on a sunny day, stood out brightly on the bare branches of a tree, Christmas leftovers. But their shiny glory was eclipsed by the rows of glistening raindrops, little balls of silver, pendant from the fingers of black branches. The gold of crisp autumn leaves had fused with the soggy red of winter. Daffodils with heads near to burst into flower were forerunners of spring in the gardens.

But the air was warming. The battle between cold and warm zones was being won by the warm air, so precipitation was taking place: gentle, persistent, gap-finding rain. I took off my gloves and realised how wet the sleeves of my coat were. I had better things to do and took a shortcut home. I switched on the central heating. I switched on the kettle. I switched on the washing machine. I switched on the TV. I switched on the computer. How easy, and how very thankfully easy. But whence the power for all this? Is Covid going to be a springboard in any way like the Great Smog(s)? Our ambitions have grown, from clean air to a cleaner climate. So coal is out and renewables are in. But, today, our local renewables were contributing nothing.

28. Winter Gardening

7 February 2021

No. of UK cases: 15,845
No. of estimated Worthing cases: 429

Years ago a friend gave me good advice as I started to get a grip on my garden, 'Plant for the winter'. The summer takes care of itself in terms of life and colour. In winter you need these even more and that requires planning ahead. Buy winter flowering or evergreen plants, she recommended.

This advice has stood me in good stead, and I am even more grateful for it in this lockdown winter. I can look around and see small red buds on brown bare branches, yellow tassels of witch hazel, variegated purple, gold and green leaves, white Christmas roses, long thin tendrils of red dogwood entwined with the green-and-yellow-striped swords of New Zealand flax, the big buds on the camellia ready to break open soon. It's not just the colour; shapes show up well too in winter: the dried heads of hydrangeas become fairytale castles when touched with frost or snow, or the blowsy seed heads of clematis, like curls of shredded wheat. And brown leaves can be touched with glory by the sun. Most years, then, I have largely left the winter garden to itself, looked on but hurried indoors. Come the end of the mowing season in the autumn, I have put the mower away and done little or nothing in the garden until the spring.

I once happened to visit Kew Gardens around this time and was amazed to see millions of crocuses in bloom in the grassy lawns of Kew. Much impressed by seeing a never-ending vista of yellow and purple, I followed suit some years later, in a small way. And from that humble beginning I do have, in the centre of the grass, a small bunch of bright yellow crocuses, which flower at the end of January.

Adding to that few has, however, proved difficult. I had a day trip to Faversham with Worthing Coaches a few years back and enjoyed a good wander around that interesting town, seeing the water-powered Gunpowder Mills (remains of) and the old quays, seeing also but walking past its most famous establishment, the Shepherd Neame Brewery. Finally, I came to the marketplace, where one stall was selling crocus plants. I bought umpteen of them but while they did well that season scarcely one has survived. The ones that do grow come up much later than the original crocuses and so I delay mowing the grass until all hope has gone.

Modern housing developments, I observe, do not have a front garden, or just sufficient to give space for the postman (and others) to deliver to the front door without risk from homebound traffic. It's the next step on from turning the front garden into hardstanding for the car. But I enjoy having a front garden as working in it is quite companionable. Cutting the front hedge especially gives opportunity for brief snatches of conversation with passers-by.

Helped along by the fact that this is the first year I have had the use of a green bin, this winter I have been more active. Keeping it filled has become a challenge just to get my money's worth. It has saved a lot of time too! Being able to trundle the bin around the garden and to toss offcuts and offshoots straight into it, especially all the prickly bits of brambles and roses has saved on effort too. The garden has certainly been the better for the bin as I have filled and put it out almost every week until about now.

Having a garden in this especially difficult year is a blessing just for a bit of space, fresh air and exercise. I am also fortunate in that, if I lean out far enough from upstairs, I can see the line of the Downs behind Worthing. Some years back I saw a remarkable time-lapse film sequence taken from space. It started off with Europe brown in the south and snowy white in the north, then from the south the green spread northwards and the north became brown, then steadily the green moved north until the north too was green. We in Worthing, when northbound over the various railway bridges of the town, can watch that change develop along the wooded line of the Downs above the town, from snowy white (occasionally) in winter, through the early yellow green of spring, to the dark green of summer, then into the autumn colours.

But, after umpteen weeks of lockdown or Tier X, short local walks have become routine and dull, yet to go further afield is not enticing. There are no cafés to go to, the supply of takeaways or coffee vans is uncertain. The usual places are crowded with people getting their deserved and much-needed fresh air. Paved area is tedious; grassy slopes like Highdown Hill have become a mudslide. But the afternoons grow a little longer and the sun creeps a little further into the garden around the corner of the house. And so, after a wet morning gave me time to remember all the items forgotten on the previous escapade and a quick walk to the shops to buy them, I returned to the garden with fresh eyes.

In estate agents' parlance, the garden is 'mostly laid to shrubs and lawn'. I am not a plants person. 'Editing' is the part I enjoy, tidying up the shrubs, keeping them in place, stopping the empire builders taking over and hopefully encouraging the half-hardy, or half-hearty, to keep at it. To ensure the garden looks as green as possible and still has life in it, the dead wood and the twiggy bits of litter must go. Also, as the grass thinks it will be greener if it grew in the border, the cutting of a sharp edge hands out a 'thus far and no farther' notice, to me if not the grass.

It was an afternoon when the weather, swinging between cold and dry one day and warm and wet the next, had managed, fortuitously, to assemble the best combination of mild and dry rather than the worst, cold and wet. I could see one or two little jobs that needed doing – and would not take long. In the summer you go out into the garden with a cup of coffee in hand and idly start dead-heading a few roses here and snipping a bit there. Before you know it, the morning has gone by, the coffee has gone cold, the pan on the hob has boiled dry, the computer is flashing angry lights.

For the final pleasure of winter gardening is that, after a couple of hours or so, the light has begun to fade, the warmth has gone from the sun, and it is time for a nice cup of tea.

29. Treats and Treatment

14 February 2021

No. of UK cases: 10,972
No. of estimated Worthing cases: 321

Last September my eyesight did not seem so good, surely, as it had been. By the end of October, I was sure my right eye was in trouble. With my left eye I could easily read the credits on TV or the subtitles, but with my right eye they were a bit fuzzy. By the time the appointment with the optometrist came (and now in Lockdown 2), car headlights at night were noticeably fuzzy. I could not convince myself that this was because of (a) dirty windscreen or (b) dirty glasses. It must be (c) 'dirty' eyes.

Wending my way through social distancing routes and sanitising rituals I met the optometrist. For years I had visited one who used traditional methods – the reading chart on the wall opposite, changing lenses from his case, working gadgetry while being close to me. But he had retired, and I was now in the modern machine set-up. It is probably more suited to Covid times and social distancing, as the need to come close is much less. Being asked to 'put my chin on the pad' was at least familiar. Thereafter, machines spat into my eyes, whizzed and whirled or sparked points of light here and there, as I made quick-fire decisions: *better? worse? here? there?* And clicked hopefully. Finally, the optometrist, who did have a traditional set of lenses open beside him, announced the eye needed treatment.

Come the due date, I thought how to get myself to the clinic. The weather forecast a fortnight out had indicated a temperature of 8°C and fairly dry, maybe with a few showers. However, by the time the day itself came, Storm Darcy and the 'Beast from the East 2' were upon us.

I had particular memories of 'Beast from the East 1' (and Storm Emma) in March 2018, when 'Beast from the East 1' dumped snow upon southern England, heavily and widely. Worthing was not so greatly affected by the snow that fell on the Thursday, but it was bitterly, miserably cold. Icy patches made walking treacherous. And I was booked for a few days holiday in Weymouth from the following Monday! But on the Friday, there were no trains beyond Bournemouth, to my great concern. The weather started to ease up late on Saturday and on the Sunday, trains were back on route, though with problems of the standard engineering type. Still, it was with some amazement I arrived in Weymouth on the Monday as planned.

And on the Tuesday, I was on the bus riding the roller coaster of the Jurassic Coast in warm sunshine, while snow still filled pockets and dips in the hills. Staying unbelievably pleasant, I got myself out to Portland Bill itself the following day by bus and walk. I sat at the café by the lighthouse celebrating, with a crab sandwich and a pot of tea, the pleasure of having a warm sun on my back, a spacious sea view and seeing the other side, the west side, of the Isle of Wight and I appreciated my good fortune.

'Beast from the East 2' had much the same dreary characteristics as Beast 1. Sunless, chill east wind, dour and dark, a few snow flurries that did nothing to enhance the scene but made paved areas slippery. Flakes of snow that did not even have the sense to fall on the ground drifted around aimlessly! I went out for a short walk and my eyes were red and weepy with cold and wind by the time I returned. I was glad when the phone rang to say the taxi was at the door. It was not the weather to ask a friend for a lift, and I was concerned about the size of the car in any case. It was a nice big car, and the young driver wore his face mask. So, we didn't have to make conversation and yet again a machine was produced to pay contactless (as we are now accustomed to say).

Having passed through the Covid rites of entry at reception: sanitise hands, don mask, temperature check, confirm my wellbeing, I sat and waited. Then, face to face, (in a manner of speaking) at least the standard face mask does not cover the eyes, the usual tests were carried out. And shortly afterwards, the poorly eye was given its treatment. I said my thanks to all for the skill, knowledge and care provided but also how I appreciated their just coming into work as required, come Covid, come Beast, come all the encumbrances Covid security requires.

And another taxi home for a welcome cup of tea. For years I drank loose leaf tea, but, seemingly being the last person to do so locally, it became unavailable to buy, and I had perforce to change to teabags. Apart from the taste, and I had found teabags I liked, it bothered me that the actual bag was not recyclable, or when put in the compost it never broke down. Having read the reviews, I had ordered leaf tea online. And the new tea had arrived just as I was down to my very last teabag. It has turned out well, with a leaf quite large, definitely not powder, and a clean, dry, fresh-off-the-bush flavour.

After 24 hours or so, I could, thankfully, read as I have not done for some time. It's not the greatest of views outside my windows, but I'm grateful to see it so well. I don't have a crab sandwich to celebrate with, but I do have the tea, lots of it, plenty to be thankful for and plenty of people to thank.

PS. I have since received confirmation that I am now inline for routine appointments and that the waiting time for the next is 45 weeks. Oh dear! That I suppose is the Covid knock-on effect. At least I shall know what to put at the top of my Father Christmas wish list.

On the Map!

22 February 2021

The Prime Minister makes a statement to the House of Commons setting out a four-step roadmap out of lockdown, with effect from 8 March.

30. Frothy Coffee

23 February 2021

No. of UK cases: 8,489
No. of estimated Worthing cases: 224

The Mayflower Steps stay in my mind as a site of courage. They were brave souls who lifted their feet from the solidity and certainty of the stone steps and put them down on the moving fluidity of a boat, then headed out of harbour for the unknown, knowing only that nothing certain lay before them. I was having a daytrip to Plymouth while staying at Paignton several years back. I wandered on and found a café selling takeaway soup and then a pleasant green square with a couple of benches overlooking the harbour. One of them was already occupied by a man who seemed more of a 'tramp' than 'homeless'. He and his dog sat there quietly enough, and I took the other bench. From another entrance into the square came a young man, possibly in clerical garb, who walked over to the tramp and offered him a cup of coffee. The tramp accepted it graciously enough and the young man walked off in a self-conscious, self-righteous manner.

The tramp came over to me and asked in a pleasant voice whether I would like the coffee. He explained that he didn't really like 'the frothy stuff' and, any case, he had his bottle of beer with him. Frothy coffee is not my favourite coffee either and I had the soup, but accepted it with, I trust, similar grace. I half-hoped that he would leave, that another would enter the square and I would be able to pass 'the frothy stuff' on to them. But that didn't happen. So I drank the coffee, said goodbye to the tramp, complimented him on his dog and its glossy coat and went my way, wondering whether the same scenario would have worked out if the young man had offered tea to the tramp. Coffee is more expensive than tea but, not only that, it is somehow more prestigious than tea, more worthy of being a gift.

Coffee and coffee bars with their noble tradition of sociability entered my life seriously, I suppose in the Swinging Sixties, when I started to frequent the Wimpy Bar and Kenco Coffee Houses, particularly the one in Kingston. Weren't we just swells then, with our bouffant hairstyle (which suited me) and miniskirts (which did not)! Really living the high life. We had stepped into a public life outside the family. And with it a desire for a better coffee at home. It was all so different from the Camp Coffee of my childhood, with its bitter taste and black, gooey semi-liquid that glugged from the bottle with its colourful label memorialising Victorian colonial wars.

Every coffee drinker has their own personal history of coffee-making equipment. Octagonal Moka pots, Melitta filters, Rombouts, all struggling to cope with the problem of coffee grounds. The simplest being a jug with coffee strainer, and in its advanced form the filter coffee system, or a cafetière with inbuilt strainer. The problem with cafetières is that, usually being made of glass, when dropped they break easily. So I relied on charity shops to keep me supplied and the coffee flowing.

Meanwhile, foreign travel brought us the pleasure of sitting outside watching the world go by. Maybe back home we didn't have the weather, the colourful Italian buildings, not quite the Italian fashion, or the spaciousness of a Roman piazza. But we spilled from the coffee houses to the outside, the pavements, the streets, the pedestrian precinct, the shopping malls. Modern Italian coffee bars, with their gaggle of gadgetry, brought us even better coffee and a new profession, that of 'barista'. The domestic version arrived in the shops and in due course into the charity shops.

And so, just before Lockdown 1, I spent all of £6 in my favourite charity shop on an espresso coffee machine! It was so old that not only was it not in the manufacturers' current catalogue; it was not even in his back catalogue. Which was a pity as there were no instructions. But pretty obvious what to do. Water in the top, coffee grounds in the middle, and from below came spurting out the golden liquid itself into the glass carafe that had miraculously survived the years. A limited amount of steam came from the steam wand but only as a leftover from the whole process. As lockdowns came and went, and cafés shut, opened and shut again, so I could, to some degree, drown my sorrows in reasonably good coffee.

But it was good coffee of its time. Standards had risen. What was now required was a good crema on the coffee; not only should the milk be frothy but the coffee itself frothy too. I found out that, to get a good crema, a pressure of at least 9 bar is needed. Mine was only 3.5, and, although I am not an enthusiast of frothy coffee, I do like hot milk with some degree of froth. So it was no great loss when the coffee machine no longer worked. Like the great coffeehouse chains, Caffe di Me (or Café de Me) was closed for business.

However, the sun was shining, 'Beast from the East 2' had cleared away and I felt in deep need of retail therapy. I had taken the lockdown month of January seriously, quite nervous about the new Kent[41] variant and encouraged to stay home by the weather. But now, with the vaccine jab giving some reassurance, I could once again enjoy the pleasure of being out in reasonable weather, without having my face and eyes bitten by a chill wind.

I could partake again in the public world of moving here and there, though sadly there would be no coffee houses as a goal. The fridge was bare and surely it was weeks since I had had a really Big Shop! And so, having filled the car full of goodies I had almost forgotten about, I went on to the click and collect to pick up the new coffee machine. Not allowed entry into the shop, of course, a table defended the entrance to which the ordered items were brought from the Aladdin's Cave within. And, while I was thereabouts, I visited the small garden centre, not only for the life-giving properties of smelling and seeing green plants but to take it home in the form of a couple more plants. Oh, and also to the pharmacist. Four shops in one day!

My understanding of my shopping strategy since lockdown began last March was that I had been to a local small convenience store weekly, to a medium supermarket fortnightly, which replaced the weekly trip, and to a Big Supermarket once a month; altogether say four times a month, five at the most. As payment had been plastic every time, cash having been made unwelcome, I could check. Surprise, surprise! I had been into a shop on average seven times a month! So now I had only three shopping days left for the next three weeks, to keep down even to that average!

---

41 The Kent variant was later renamed the Alpha variant.

At home again I faced up to the new technology. Three buttons to press and a dial to turn. My goodness this thing is clever! But it has an instruction book. And so, I came to the section on cleaning and maintenance! 'Descaling': what's that? It had never occurred to me to do that to the old machine. Perhaps that was all that was wrong with it. If I descaled it, would it work again? I could then check it in again at a charity shop in due course, taking all the other things that had missed their chance in various lockdowns, and it could continue on its way. Meanwhile, as I have become more handy with using the new machine, out of it does come coffee with a very good crema and an impressive froth and foam. Hurrah for barista me! So, while we continue to be denied the sociable aspect of good coffee, I can at least enjoy the stuff itself, though the skill of making a pretty pattern in the froth so far eludes me.

Sociability has been provided as I have walked along the seafront, enjoying not just exercise but the pleasure of being out in others' company, not just the family's company but of the world in general; of people we don't know. Maybe as we walk together, or zoom around, we have learned a little more of the art and skill to talk to people to whom we have not been introduced, to go beyond family enclosure, that unseen perimeter closely guarding our personal world; to leave the safe houses of our habitual life and step into the unknown of other people's company, values and interests. Is this the Covid spirit? Maybe, when we can once more sit outside and not only watch the world go by, we might even talk to it as well.

From last evening's announcements of the timeline out of lockdown, we can now look forward to that more certainly but, as another sailor out of Plymouth, Francis

Drake,[42] wrote, 'There must be a beginning of any great matter, but the continuing unto the end until it be thoroughly finished yields the true glory.'

42 Letter to Sir Francis Walsingham, from off Cape Sagres, Portugal (17 May 1567), https://en.wikiquote.org/w/index.php?title=Francis_Drake&oldid=2992128 (last visited 2 January 2022).

31. Smile Please!

1 March 2021

No. of UK cases: 5,455
No. of estimated Worthing cases: 102

Lunch in the garden in February! Warm sunshine; light wind. Just glad to be out in the garden after days indoors with the central heating on, or outdoors in a cruel wind. Glad of the space without having to leave home, and grateful for it. Anyone would think I had not been down to the seafront or off to the shops as occasion required. It feels as if we have been under house arrest for months, but only another few weeks and we will be let out! It may only be for something like day release (and lunch with another outside), and then on parole for three months. But winter itself is the great jailer and 1 March the day when meteorologists declare it spring. Why they can't wait another three weeks like everyone else they don't explain. If it is because they are tidy-minded and want the seasons to start on the first of a month, you would think they would have chosen the following first of the month rather than the preceding. Ideally, winter should start as late as possible, 1 January, but spring as soon as possible, 1 March!

Anyway, lunch in the garden in February, even if I am wearing a winter coat and beginning to wonder if it was such a good idea. But also hurrying through lunch to get on with the jobs around the garden that immediately demanded attention. Not only is it good for the garden to have me doing things it is good for me in general and, in particular, it is good for my eyes. They have spent too much time looking at computers and TV and being dried out by the central heating inside and by the wind outside, and the cold. So, they are sore, red and irritable and extra sensitive to light as a by-product, even though I have been slopping in eye drops.

Meanwhile, when out, I have in the shops at any rate been wearing a face mask and, as I've got off the bus, left it on at times, either because I've forgotten or because it has suddenly become a useful protection against wind and weather. Five years back now, I came off the bus to walk home, which, in the usual way, takes a good five minutes, say: the sort of time you don't think about but just allow for when you go out to catch the bus. On that occasion, the wind blew hard from the north-east, driving nails of sleet and hail into my exposed face. I have never known the walk to be so long! In such circumstances, in this Covid winter, I could keep my face mask on, which would protect the lower half of my face, at any rate. But not my eyes.

Perhaps I should try a face visor, as I have been calling the alternative to cloth masks, but when I began the hunt for a provider realised that, in the trade, they are called 'face shields'. In fact, I could not find one available in a local shop as they seem to be available only through trade suppliers. So online and then no problem. Whereupon I found yet another decision had to be made. From choice I did not want to wear one that said FACE SHIELD writ large over my forehead. I presume this is to advise the onlooker that the wearer is doing their social duty and wearing protective gear, even if not as visible as a mask.

Also, as one who wears glasses, I was attracted to a variation that claimed to be for those who do wear glasses and, coincidentally, did not have FACE SHIELD stamped on them. During the next couple of days while waiting delivery I saw someone wearing glasses and a face shield in the standard form. However, it protruded at an angle over her spectacles so that at chin level it was several inches away from her face, which was not a good defence against Covid, I would have thought.

In due course I was in possession of a minuscule box and investigated. In a tight roll was the plastic shield and separately a pair of clear plastic glasses in effect, but frames only, with no lens to them. These 'glasses' then buttoned on to the visor, and then over my own glasses, rather like wearing two pairs. And so, I sallied forth into the garden, to do the jobs lunch had observed. It was certainly warmer inside my shield. The sun may have been shining spring, but the air was still winter chill, and the wind had increased. What I immediately found, and was slightly bothered by, was the reflection bouncing off the side of the shield. No way would it have been possible to drive the car in that, but then one is unlikely to want to wear it inside the car. So how do motorcyclists manage inside their big visors? It must be different somehow.

After a couple of hours of snipping here and pottering there, my eyes did feel that the shield had done a reasonably good job of protecting them from the wind. It was OK to wear them in the garden, but how would I feel at walking up to the shops in them? I believe face shields are not as Covid-secure as masks, but they have other advantages such as: you can breathe in them! Glasses do not steam up so much, talking is a lot easier and better. It stops you touching your eyes and nose, but it is still difficult to blow your nose! Certainly, for the time being it is socially acceptable to be out and about in them, and perhaps will be again next winter.

But if, during the summer, the requirements to wear face coverings are relaxed, perhaps it would be better to think of other ways of protecting my eyes. And the simplest way might be simply to smile! For it is not only the length of time we look at screens that is important but that tense, concentrated gaze with which we do so. I'm sure the only eye muscle I've been using is the one that keeps me looking intensely, and tensely, at the screen. So, remembering to smile more, should remedy that and benefit the eyes.

And if we are to meet friends again, how much better to meet them with a happy smile than with the deadpan look that the tedium of winter indoors has made the customary facial expression. Smiling with the eyes, I mean. It is a particular form of smile, it seems, and has a name! The Duchenne smile,[43] after the 19th-century French neurologist Guillaume Duchenne, who investigated the physiology of emotions. There are, of course, videos about technique on YouTube, and exercises on Wikihow on how to attain the Duchenne smile.

It makes you smile!

43   Smile, https://en.wikipedia.org/w/index.php?title=Smile&oldid=1060194133 (last visited 22 December 2021).

from 8 March 2021

People can meet one person from another household for recreation but must maintain social distancing.

32. Garden Art

8 March 2021

No. of UK cases: 4,712
No. of estimated Worthing cases: 226

Why are they called 'landscape painters'? They're painting canvases like anyone else. Not like street artists, who are painting the street. It's the same difference between portrait painters and face-painting. So what am I doing? Aren't I doing landscape painting? I stepped out from the bushes to take a good look, and, from underneath my sheepdog hairstyle, surveyed the work. So far, I had painted about a quarter of one of the panels of my long fence and painted it brown. Brown as it has always been, except for the unfortunate time I found the shop sold two browns and I had bought the other one, which went on like tinned tomatoes. There was enough left of proper brown to mix the two together to some extent and create a gradient effect: proper brown at one end, morphing into tomato brown at the other. It was the outside, fortunately, so it wasn't me who saw it.

But I was feeling corralled, caught inside the fence, not quite running up and down inside it like a caged animal, but pretty near. It is still another month before we can leave the local area and I'm weary of the usual local walks. The feeling of confinement has been increased as efforts to break out in other ways have been thwarted. For example, when telephoning a company, the automatic voice replies, 'We are currently experiencing high volumes of calls and all our colleagues are busy. Please be assured your message is important to us and a colleague will reply as soon as one is available.' When emailing, the automatic reply comes 'We are currently experiencing high volumes of emails. Please be assured your message is important to us…' I wrote a letter and posted it to a London address. It took six weeks before it was even delivered! Snail mail indeed!

Why always a brown fence? A revolution was brewing. The fence is brown because it's wood, and brown is a good background colour for shrubs and plants to show up against, as and when they flower. The theory is not to draw attention to it. But maybe that's wrong. Maybe it would be better to camouflage it by painting it the colour of the areas it cuts me off from, such as the sky. Or maybe, it would look further away if painted the same colour as the paths and paving, as if to extend that. Or maybe, if there are colours I like of the appropriate paint, why not use them? If I've got to look at the fence it must be worth looking at. Why should the garden look natural? What's natural? Capability Brown went in for the 'natural look' and changed the landscape around to make it so. Designer natural.

Over the next cup of coffee, I consulted the shop's paint catalogue. They had a good choice of fence colours. Why be so unadventurous painting it all one colour, and always brown? And they had tester pots for them too. A bit pricey, perhaps, but not as expensive per litre as printer ink cartridges! In fact, two to three years ago I had painted almost all the downstairs using tester pots. Because the house has chimney breasts, and walls have been knocked down here and built up there, the walls go in and out, so it was possible to paint every face a different shade of green. This despite the motto 'two greens should not be seen without another colour in between'.

I took the bus into town, not having been there since around Christmas time, that is, since the beginning of Lockdown 3, and was shocked at the ghost town it had become. It was both shocking and yet comforting that there were so few folk around. The shock was, as it were, to realise that lockdown was real, I hadn't made it all up. It was comforting that other people believed in lockdown and were taking it seriously. But essential shopping is not what town centres are about. No one goes to the town centre for such items. It's contrary to its purpose and nature. So, there were open only a few, including the hardware shop I needed. Yet, if the shops are shut and there's scarcely anyone out and around, and all the oldies like me have been jabbed, why are numbers of Covid cases in Worthing so high?

Best to get in and get out. With a collection of tester pots I came home to make sense of my purchases. I hadn't been able to get a tester pot of all the colours I really liked; others had taken those already. A good sign, in its way, but it meant the ones I hadn't were the ones I probably wanted. It would be nice to know.

Perhaps 'garden art' is a better description than 'landscape painting', for the other form it takes is painting with water! Or is that a form of carving? Sculptors are said to see the form they want to reveal within the block of stone they have before them. Similarly, pressure-washing the paths and patios cuts through the mud and grime and discolouration to reveal the true colour underneath, or what's left of it. It's very satisfying, if a bit cold on the feet with all the water sloshing around. It's a slow job too, standing in parts of the garden where the sun doesn't reach this time of the year, though I have stayed out late enough to realise how the sun has moved on, and now sets spreading red and gold behind the bare black branches of big trees down the road.

Last time I paid a couple of guys – Bright Spark and the lad – to clean the paths and rather more. Half-way through the job, Bright Spark picked an argument and stalked off, the lad following on. I had paid up front – how foolish can one get? As one gets older, one finds out! But it wasn't all loss. The lad had done 9/10 of the cleaning and, later, I found he had left his cable extension, and also a really good connector on the hose!

Decision time on what colours to put where, and when! Wonderful how a walk in the crisp spring air clears the brain and cheers the mind. Plan A is to paint the panels in the lower half of the fence alternately darkish grey and green but to divide panels in the upper half into four squareish sections and paint each a different pale colour: pale blue, pink, green and natural. Or is that just blue-sky thinking?

33. 20...21... and Counting

15 March 2021

No. of UK cases: 5,089
No. of estimated Worthing cases: 343

Forty years ago, almost to the day, I stood in the town hall in a queue working its way up the staircase and started chatting to the person on the step above me. We were there as would-be enumerators for the 1981 census, ready to take delivery of the Field Manual, the necessary paperwork, and to attend the briefing session.

I was an enumerator in both the 1981 and 1991 censuses. These required me, as far as I remember, in the first instance to deliver the census forms to the 200 or so households of my patch, to contact preferably the householder, explain to them who should be recorded even if temporarily absent, and answer any queries. By and large there was no problem but there were the recluses, as I called them: people who opened the front door sufficient to get their head round, took the form, and shut the door in my face. When I collected it, they handed me the form without speaking, and shut the door again. There were also those who said they would have to consult their solicitor before filling in the form. Confident of the solicitor's answer, I left them to spend the money!

I made arrangements to give out or pick up forms at 2130 at night or 0800 in the morning. I went to one house and pressed the bell; no one came, the house was empty, but the bell went on ringing. As I closed the gate, I could hear the bell still ringing. I ran away! When a woman said that her husband was in hospital, I talked about temporary absences, saying, brightly, that that was no problem; he should still be included. She looked at the date and said, calmly, 'He'll be dead by then.'

There was another briefing session about the collection of the forms, before the actual Census Day. There were empty houses I had to check to see whether they were still empty, or whether people had come back at the last minute and should be included. Somebody had indeed turned up, only I'd forgotten to bring the form with me! And it was really cold day too for doing the double journey. Then it was a rush to get all the forms back, variously check them on the door, check them again at home, and go back with queries.

Gradually I whittled down the numbers of outstanding forms, again, as necessary, visiting at strange hours of the day. A pub was on my circuit on the 1981 census, with a live-in barman. The first evening I went, he said he had not completed the form. I suspected he was standing me up! Second evening I went back, he served everybody at the bar while I stood by, then said the bar was so busy he couldn't leave it to collect the form from his flat. I was sure he was standing me up. Third evening I went back with my male supervisor. At once the young man went back to his flat for the form!

It was embarrassing if you found someone on your area whom you knew personally but obviously didn't want to know their details. In those cases, you gave them a special envelope and they put the form in and sealed it.

Some people, like the recluses, wanted that anyway. Or there might be someone in the household who wanted to keep their own details private, and they were then given their own individual form. Finally, having done all the paperwork, I had to do the paperwork to say I had done the paperwork, and hand it all in. For all my checking and rechecking, I had still overlooked one omission, so had to return to ask a householder to put in the date of birth of his wife. I wondered if she ever received birthday cards and presents!

Little me should have made her first entry onto the census in the 1941 census, except that that was not held because of the War.[44] However, the National Register was established, a system of identity cards and instant census, on 29 September 1939.[45] I was on it from its beginning! I still remember my National Registration number. It was in the form ABCD123/4, and it became my NHS number when the NHS started in 1948. It could still have a use as a computer password – the only one I would remember.

The 1991 census was the last time the census was carried out in the traditional manner, developed over 150 years, pre-computer, pre-internet, pre-smartphone. Murmuring was already starting about the value and cost of the census. And so, in 2001, the census forms were delivered by enumerators but returned by post.[46] Then, in

---

44   Census in the United Kingdom, https://en.wikipedia.org/w/index.php?title=Census_in_the_United_Kingdom&oldid=1043154083 (last visited 22 December 2021).

45   National Registration Act 1939, https://en.wikipedia.org/w/index.php?title=National_Registration_Act_1939&oldid=1033796114 (last visited 22 December 2021).

46   2001 United Kingdom Census, https://en.wikipedia.org/w/index.php?title=2001_United_Kingdom_census&oldid=1059100770 (last visited 31 December 2021).

2011,[47] the form came by post and was returned by post or could be submitted online. All that has come to us in the post for the 2021 census has been a letter giving a magic number and an explanatory leaflet. These are our starting point to complete the Census online, a word that would have been meaningless when I last was an enumerator! Given the Covid pandemic it is probably fortunate that the old method has been abandoned.

The first census I filled in in my own name was the 1961 census, when I had just moved to London, and I remember the pride I took in doing so, and still do. As one gets older, the chances of completing yet another decennial census diminish. I must take the opportunity and go online and try to work my way through it all. I hope.

47   2011 United Kingdom Census, https://en.wikipedia.org/w/index. php?title=2011_United_Kingdom_census&oldid=1062108866 (last visited 31 December 2021).

34. Clock On

29 March 2021

No. of UK cases: 4,654
No. of estimated Worthing cases: 63

The change to British Summer Time is a bit of a palaver that we do once each way, each year. But, during WW2 there was British *Double* Summer Time! As a child, I had nothing to do with changing the clocks. I just remember the struggle of trying to get to sleep in a west-facing bedroom when sunset was not until 2230 or thereabouts, in the height of summer. British Summer Time started early in 1940,[48] on 25 February, but in the autumn the clocks were not put back. In spring

---

48   British Summer Time, https://en.wikipedia.org/w/index.php?title=British_Summer_Time&oldid=1061446918 (last visited 22 December 2021).

1941 the clocks went another hour forward but only that hour was taken off in the autumn. GMT did not return until the autumn change of clocks in 1945.

'Summer Time' in winter was tried again between October 1968 and October 1970.[49] I remember the misery of going to work in the dark, and then coming home in the dark as well, and was much relieved when Parliament overwhelmingly voted against continuing the practice. There are eight hours of daylight in midwinter (in southern England) and fiddling around with clock time does not change that.

Changing the clocks then was easy! They were all analogue and mechanical and you simply pushed the hands around to the right time, though it was deemed wise not to push them back in the autumn. I suppose the clock for the central heating system (we didn't have that during the war; no way) has the same simplicity. But what else? The clock in the car is one press for one minute so I have to press it umpteen times to change the time, especially in the autumn. It may be fall back not spring forward but it means forwarding by 23 hours. On the clock on the kitchen cooker, I have to turn the knob anticlockwise to make the hands move, well, clockwise. If not, it upsets the automatic timing system and strange noises happen, or the oven comes on or the grill won't work!

Everything else is digital. The phones need the instructions for the combination of asterisks, hashkeys and numbers, let alone the time. I now have that information copied in enlarged form so that, by the time I've worked my way through the process, time hasn't moved on from what I've set it at. And with the current set of phones, you change only the one and it tells the others what do.

49   As previous footnote.

Smartphones and computers seem to know for themselves what to do.

But there is always some clock or watch or digi device that you never even knew had a clock attached to it that somehow gets forgotten. Only the arrival at an unearthly hour of the postman knocking, or the wheelie bins being trundled around brings you up to speed. One year I forgot completely about changing the clock in the spring, and turned up for lunch just as the hosts and other guests had reached the pudding stage! Alternatively, it was embarrassing, as the host in the autumn, when a guest turned up early, in that precious last hour when more needs to be done than there is time available for!

Everyone has their own mark of when spring or summer starts for real for them, whether it is a particular plant that flowers in the garden or the buds on a tree show. For me, it is when the sun comes through the garden door again for the first time since September and there appears a small patch of brightness on the dark receiving wall. It grows bigger and bigger and penetrates into the room further and further amazingly quickly. It happens just a few days before the equinox and requires a really sunny late afternoon and sunset. Some years I feel deprived as I wait hopefully for the wonder to reappear, but cloud or bad weather prevents it happening on the due date.

It looks this year as if we shall have appropriate weather for the start of summertime, with the forecast of really warm sunny days in the forthcoming week. So often the change in the clocks has little to do with the weather and we have to endure for another two to three weeks an extra hour of looking at cold, cloudy, white skies when we can't decently draw the curtains, or put the fire on, before the weather catches up with the date.

It's a curious month, March anyway, named after the Roman god of War, Mars. The aphorism 'in like a lion, out like lamb' or vice versa fits it well, or at least recognises that March is a double-edged month. It is even more a two-way month than January, named after the two-headed Roman god Janus, who looked back and forth. January is just a steady descent into cold and darkness. In March, one day we are in winter and then suddenly spring, if not summer weather, is upon us.

This year in particular, March is a two-way month. We have looked back to the beginning of Covid a year ago, when the phrase 'social distancing' first entered the language early in March 2020. Not knowing quite what lay ahead, we bought up the UK's supply of toilet rolls. Like locusts in the harvest field, we descended on the supermarkets and scoured the shelves before lockdown proper began on 23 March.

In some crisis of the early 1990s – when the Chancellor stood out in Downing Street and brushed back his quiff of white hair – I passed the local electrician's shop – shut – and read the notice on the door, 'The light at the end of the tunnel has, for economy reasons, been switched off.' This was much my feeling when Lockdown 3 was announced at the start of the new year. But now, Covid-weary and lockdown-hardened, the light is back on in a flickering sort of way, or at least we have a finger on the switch.

And we appreciate getting out and about even more. And so, having looked back, we can look forward also to summertime and to a rather more certain, more relaxed summer than last year, beginning with a bit of sociability in friends' and neighbours' gardens. Weather permitting and getting the time right.

April – On Track

from 12 April 2021

No more than 6 people can meet and outdoors only

Non-essential retail, personal care services, indoor leisure facilities and public libraries can reopen.

Restaurants and pubs can open for outdoor service.

35. Not Yet Normal

12 April 2021

No. of UK cases: 3,568
No. of estimated Worthing cases: 80

My fingers keep fiddling with a length of over long, or overheavy hair just behind my ear. BUT I am determined not to cut my hair! Hopefully, I shall get to the hairdresser this coming week, and the theory is to leave enough hair around for them to establish a reasonable average. So, I am trying not to fiddle, though it is like trying not to scratch an itch.

I had missed my chance last autumn or perhaps, as restrictions eased, I had become accustomed again to going to the hairdresser as required. For whatever reason it was, I was caught out. Just as my hair did need to be cut, down came the grilles, the shutters, the gates were closed, the doors locked.

The refinements of delicate snipping and shaping with which I had whiled away a Sunday afternoon last summer required too much patience in the boredom and frustrations of Lockdown 3. I had found a good sharp pair of scissors with a crisp bite to them and boldly cut. Two things only guided me – firstly, if I could see long, lanky hair in the wrong place, and, secondly, if I could feel long, lanky hair in the wrong place. I hoped it would come out fairly well around the back but didn't over care about that detail. And, when I went out, I mostly wore a cap or hat in any case.

And where to go to? I am weary of drinking coffee from cardboard cups from coffee vans, standing around awkwardly with or without company, or sitting in a row not quite hearing what the end of the line was saying. Never will sitting up to table seem so agreeable or looking across to another so welcome. I did once have a refectory table only 2ft wide – that was looking too closely into the eyes of the person opposite!

But then the phone call came last Friday. I did have somewhere to go to. I could go to the surgery and have my second jab! Much relieved and excited, as I had noticed how time was closing in on the 12 weeks from my first jab at the end of January. In fact, there were only four days left. I had been five millionth (give or take) to have the first jab; now I would be seven millionth (give or take) to have the second. Where had all these interlopers come from?

So to the surgery on a Saturday afternoon. I had had the choice of an early-morning appointment but, as before, had taken the teatime alternative. This time it was not in the dark, nor as cold. The car park was also a little more organised, with a ropeway to guide me along the way and friendly volunteers from thereon to check me in, find me a seat, find better seats for others, offer a helping hand as needed. But it was very quiet. There wasn't the chatter of the first time, or the excitement and buzz that had accompanied us on our progress through the process. In fact, it was like sitting in the doctor's waiting room, only for some reason we were sitting in the corridor, socially distanced.

I heard my first name called, but slightly doubted the second name, yet stood up hopefully. Then from another area another walked forward slowly, leaning heavily on her walking sticks, who had a better claim. I waited longer, and then heard my first name, and surely my second name too. But another stood up, a man. I suggested I had a more convincing claim to be the person named and he gracefully withdrew and sat down.

And so, into the large room where about four stations were set out. I offered my card with details of my first appointment on it to the nurse 'jabber', while her colleague at the computer checked my name. The jabber then went through the ritual of asking was I suffering from anything Covid related. Thankfully, I was not. Duly jabbed, and my card returned now marked also with the details of my second jab, I walked to the room for 15 minutes' meditation. Maybe that should become standard practice at the doctor's.

The volunteer in charge was rather more outgoing than at the first jab and checked that everyone leaving had done their time. But also rang for a taxi for two of the patients, which seemed going beyond the call of duty. And so, home again. I shall keep my card as a souvenir. Some time we shall be out of all this or as far as we're ever going to be. The not yet normal has made a start, at least.

Meanwhile, my hair is growing, and I must away to the hairdresser. I trust they are looking forward to the challenge.

36. The Baffling Bourne

19 April 2021

No. of UK cases: 2,963
No. of estimated Worthing cases: 32

First coach out of Worthing for months and first row in the coach, which means, in these not yet normal times, the second row, but still a good view of the open road ahead. Not because of my choice but because good Covid practice as practised by Worthing Coaches requires the first people to step aboard to sit at the back and the last people to come on to have the front seats. Not many people on the coach anyway. So why was I not feeling quite as joyous as you would expect? Because it was neither back to proper normal nor the first time out of lockdown. That was last summer. We've been here before. And nobody gets excited by second attempts. I am also going to a place I have visited before.

But a lovely sunny morning in a chilly way as the coach turned into the Rownhams Service Station near Southampton. I like service stations, full of the bustle and tension of people on the move, getting this, wanting that, needing a break but also wanting to get on. Not really like that this morning, not even a queue at the ladies'. One-way arrows stuck on the floor guided us in and out of our chosen coffee provider. I took my coffee to the outside area and the sunshine and caffeine cheered me up. Thus the flat calm green fields of the Sussex coast gave way to waves of yellow gorse rolling to the far horizon as we crossed the spaciousness of the New Forest, through the village of Lyndhurst, between tall trees, and into Bournemouth.

It is not the place that gets my heart beating and imagination flowing. A couple of years ago I had spent a short holiday in Bournemouth and had used most of my time going somewhere else, like Poole, taking the chain ferry to the Isle of Purbeck, or going the other way to Hengistbury Head[50] and Christchurch. But to go to a place only half-known has one advantage. I could recognise where we were when the coach stopped and would not need the first few minutes to get my whereabouts, or which way up to hold the map.

Yet Bournemouth baffles me. There's no old town to explore. There's no harbour. There are no old buildings to wonder at. Nothing historic happened here. Nobody famous came here to make it famous. Is it just famous for being famous? How come it is such a big city with amazing new multicoloured, multiclad, multistoried buildings in its suburbs? There's the fascinating Russell-Cotes Museum[51] on the East Cliff, which I had visited some time back and another visit, Covid permitting, would most pleasurably occupy me.

I needed to do a few humdrum pieces of shopping, so went up the east side hill to the shopping centre there, but to complete the purchases had to come down that hill and go up the west side hill. It was certainly a welcome sight

---

50   Hengistbury Head, https://www.hengistbury-head.co.uk.
51   Russell-Cotes, https://russellcotes.com.

to see people sitting outside of cafés in the pedestrianised area, as now allowed, and plenty more strolling around. On my stay here, I had seen, at beach leaving time, hordes of people flowing homewards through the Gardens. Maybe Bournemouth is always full of people.

But having done my bit of shopping it was time for lunch. This was not to be a celebratory sit-up-to-table knife-and-fork meal with a friend. That was in the diary but not for today. I had my sandwiches with me but would like them accompanied by hot soup. But old-fashioned, nourishing hot soup can be surprisingly difficult to come by. And, in this area of smart cafés, perhaps out of place. I tried without success a few side roads.

I wandered down the hill to take an interest, for the first time, in the flat land between the two hills. The Lower Gardens. With chairs and tables out and customers about, surely one of the several small cafés and kiosks would do soup. No way. Parks & Gardens flower beds filled the area, white hyacinths, red polyanthus and blue forget-me-nots at measured distances, a long low-walled rockery, the noisy birds of the aviary, the band stand, the mini-golf. Huge pine trees around, carefree squirrels cheekily crossing one's path. It was all the epitome of a well-kept, well-bred seaside town park.

And, equally well under control, trapped between its stone lined walls, was a little stream running down the middle. Yet it fought against its limits, flowing fast, falling over little weirs, tumbling unbalanced over stones and obstacles in its hurrying way. Whence came this rough disturbing energy? Maybe it would lead me into a 'rough' hot-soup-making area? I turned and headed towards its source, wherever that was. I crossed the largely pedestrianised square into the Central Gardens.

Here stood the pergola bridge, huge redwoods, a horse chestnut beginning to shake off winter. The impressive Cenotaph. Not so many people hereabouts. I looked hopefully outside the gardens at the accompanying roads. Would any of these provide hot soup? Far from it. Large splendacious 1930s blocks of apartments enjoyed the view.

A final chance: the last café was signed. No soup. I gave in, and settled for coffee, and a view of a few brave players playing on what looked like 'grass' courts. But it was chilly; the cloud cover had thickened; a few drops of rain pockmarked the path. At least I could eat up and move on. Outdoor eating requires suitable outdoor weather, and this was not such. But a huge green 'polytunnel' intrigued me, more of a cloche than a tunnel, to be sure. Was this where they nurtured their big trees? No, it contained, as I peeked through the 'glass' window, indoor tennis courts.

I walked underneath Wessex Way, carrying its endless flow of noisy traffic, and into the Upper Gardens. Not so domesticated as the Lower Gardens as tidy-minded gardeners were beginning to lose control. No neat flower beds, but big trees, big shrubs, wide grassed borders to the stream still rushing between stone walls, but its power was beginning to tell on them. I came upon a charming little folly, a lone Gothic tower complete with castellation, a turret in one corner and arrow-slits in the main body of the building.

I came to a sign to the Coy Pond, but with no indication of how far to walk or what it was. Coy, could that be short for Decoy or was it another spelling of Koi fish? The stream was still flowing steadily and strongly, but now through natural grassy banks. What a change of scenery! This was the Wild Wood or, more exactly, the Wild Wet Wood and Gardens. The stream slowed, barely to be distinguished from the boggy marshy area through which it meandered. A duckboard path covered in netting let one pass just inches above the sodden earth, among triffid like ferns, plants like uncoiling seahorses, yellow celandines, cornflower-blue flowers, white allium. Weeping willows wept copiously.

I was becoming uneasy about how time and the walk had drifted on and how far I was from 'home base'. Still, I pressed on, giving myself a time limit of when I should turn back, with or without discovering the Coy Pond. Yet more huge redwoods with their distinctive soft fibrous bark towered above the general greenery.

But sunlight appeared around me, the area opened out into a modern housing area and, while the stream and grassy slopes continued a little further left, on my right was the Coy Pond! Gaudy mallards paddled happily around or slid down from the island into the dark water. Young children were entranced by a green-and-white moth warming in the sun on an equally green and mottled lichen covered rail. And at the far end a fountain of water poured out from an equally huge hole through a slalom of red-brick walls into the pond. This was it. The End. I could walk no farther. Beyond and above was a road and housing. But still no answer to my question, 'whence this rough disturbing energy?' In any case, it was time I headed back.

But I had not gone far, past bug hotels and a bug city, when I was 'stumped'. I had come across a 'stumpery',[52] a Victorian enthusiasm here recreated. A collection of old fern stumps, tree stumps, cut-down large branches were piled together at one side. But there was the other stretch

---

52 Stumpery, https://en.wikipedia.org/w/index.php?title=Stumpery&oldid=991013204 (last visited 26 December 2021).

of water; into this the Coy Pond poured. The yellow gravel path on which I had latterly approached the pond continued a little further, but then it too surrendered to nature, so I walked on grass to... where? Another hole, another stream of water outpouring, but from a steep wooded slope. The End again! I had to go, and walked past an old and lovely house built in the Italianate style, swages of grapes and laurel decorated the stonework, and a pergola set against the side of the house.

It did take me nearly an hour to walk back to Bournemouth and the Lower Gardens, and so to the next question: where is the Mouth of the Bourne? Where does it debouche into the sea? Just where an underpass for pedestrians opens up, and while the traffic from West Cliff to East Cliff passes overhead, the Bourne enters the nether world to flow on its own subterranean passage. But when I followed the pedestrian walk through to the prom, the sea, the pier, there was no sign of the Bourne stream, no cut through of the beach, no obvious merging with the wide ocean. Its end was as mysterious as its beginning. No doubt I could ask the helpful tourist office but perhaps some things should be left unasked.

It is always pleasing to come home with a mystery, and a reason to visit again, and I look forward to visiting Bournemouth again. And a whole season of such trips was now open to me, Covid permitting.

37. Out of Cash

27 April 2021

No. of UK cases: 2,685
No. of estimated Worthing cases: 13

It showed how out of practice we were! With the celebratory sit-up-to-table, knife-and-fork meal (outside) with a friend having ended, I paid by card, as did my friend. She then looked at me and said, 'What about the tip? Do you have any cash?' Cash! What's that?

Years after everyone else began to use the 'hole in the wall', I edged my card for the first time into the allotted gape of the machine, watched as it slid out of sight and nervously waited for ever before it smoothly slid back into my world and my grasping hand again. Before then I had collected the OAP in cash from the Post Office and paid what was left of it into the bank. Thus, I kept two institutions going. But then, in the ungrateful way that progress has, the letter came from Them to say I should transfer to a bank paying-in arrangement. At much the same time, the bank I had used for years closed down. So, in an unenthusiastic way, I became accustomed to cash from the machine, assuming, that is, that it has the money, and in the denomination needed, and is not going to charge me for wanting my own cash.

Now, after a year and more of Covid, I can hardly remember when I did use the machine. Crisp bank notes have stayed untouched in the back of my purse for months. Cash is no longer king. Plastic is, and preferably contactless. And for ever smaller amounts. Years ago, I was buying some wine from a convenience store, and was told the minimum free pay by card was £15. I objected and the assistant then put the extra out of his own pocket into the till. Very embarrassing. Then, maybe in the year pre-Covid, another shopkeeper in another shop was expressing his amazement that the young would pay for even less than £1 by card. But I did that last week, and nobody blinked an eye.

However, situations remain when you do need cash, and small change in particular. Like tipping the hairdresser, or the taxi driver. You can add it to the card, if you remember in time, but it never seems as satisfactory. One leaves, hoping the person intended does get the dosh. In any case, you cannot tip the coach driver that way, should you so wish.

You need a coin for the supermarket trolley. You can buy the token from one supermarket and have it handy for all of them, until you lose it or don't have it with you. Failing all else, I suppose you could tip the hairdresser (female?) with it; she might recognise its worth. But the coach driver (male?) would probably look quite baffled. If the world goes short of cash, will they just lose out? Do I need to tip? What have they done that is not part of the job, what they are paid for? Personal service, friendly helpful people, individual attention. Would they be in the job if they weren't or didn't?

Kindly people also dribble coins into charity collecting pots on supermarket tills, or on shop counters. Volunteers shake buckets around on street corners awaiting whatever passers-by can quickly draw out from pockets or purses. That scenario has been disturbed by Covid not only because of cash problems but because of social distancing and more. Technology has kicked in again, though, with text funding, where you add a 5 to a number and so donate £5 to the good cause. The account I have is probably not the right kind to do that, I think. Crowd funding for a cause that catches the eye and the imagination is possible only through social media. Then there are the organisations that take the problem of the actual handling (and counting) dirty Covid-infected cash away from the organiser and possibly the embarrassment of knowing another's generosity.

You can pay at the petrol station for petrol by card, but if you need to put air in the tyres you need a coin, or coins. It is as if air wasn't nothing but a something. Indeed, I know it is a something, as my first bike had solid rubber tyres. It was my best birthday present ever to have a bicycle with pneumatic tyres, not rubber holding me up but air.

You need coins for the car park pay and display. Or you can be cunning and mean and master the rules for your home turf and which road (and which side of the road) is free for how long, on what days. Of course, they say it backwards to you, i.e., they give the hours you can't park, which is fairly baffling to residents and totally mystifying to visitors.

Now, post-12 April, the buses are offering to give change if you are not paying by card or pass. They did not do this during lockdown, when either you paid the right money or paid by card or pass. Not so much because they could not get the change, I think, but because they did not want their drivers to handle Covid-filthy lucre.

The coin for which there is no alternative, however, is when you need 20p for the ladies'. I sympathise with those small town councils who generously provide public conveniences, who keep them clean, serviced and usable but for whom the charge on their budgets is significant. Yet, somehow, it seems an affront to one's human rights.

Years back, when the threat was to cease cheques, I think 2018 was the date, the concern was what people at home would do when they needed to pay the plumber, or to send away for a subscription or to make a donation. Maybe the concern was not so much the difficulty for the house owner but the fear on the part of Them that the payment would be in cash, and not go through the books at all. But, with online technology, bank transfers have largely become routine between individuals as much as organisations. And I have managed that!

In these Covid times, they want you not to visit the bank. Even if it still there to visit. But I shall need to go. Then to take one of the fresh crispy notes given on the outside of the bank into the inside, to have it changed into money. I mean real money, cash. I want the promise to pay on demand honoured, right there and then.

But I'm out of date, as ever. 'Pay and display' at the car park? No cash, no problem: 'pay by mobile'! So, will that happen at the ladies'? Possibly, the kind of council that does charge does not have the resources to put in the wherewithal to bring that about. That gives me time to find out the cleverness that you have to do to 'pay by mobile'.

38. Poll Position

10 May 2021

No. of UK cases: 2,357
No. of estimated Worthing cases: 12

Walking across the park to the polling station used to be, for me, part of the ritual of voting. It gave opportunity to arrive 'with heart and mind prepared', as another tradition would put it. Joining the queue, if any, was to meet up with other members of the community in exercising and maintaining our democratic rights and duties. Then I became a poll clerk, sitting the other side of the table. Mostly I was not assigned to 'my' station but to another local station in another church hall.

I enjoyed walking there also around 0615 to give time to set the station up for the 0700 opening. At that time of day, some houses had no lights on at all, some had bedroom lights on only and some had lights on both upstairs and downstairs. And, of course, there were already dog walkers heading to or even home from the park.

But, as I was not at my own station, I needed a postal vote, so filled in the required forms and received the pack, and the instructions. Like many a DIY manual, when you have put it all together you understand the instructions. They sound tedious and complicated but, as one works one's way through, their sense and the process becomes clear. Usually, I took the completed forms back into the town hall. It both saved the town a few pennies and again maintained that sense of taking part in the process for real.

One year I tried my hand at the count. I was hopeless! Everyone else in the team was, I imagine, a cashier from a bank or such. I was so slow! I could feel the irritation of the team growing as I laboriously turned and counted the voting slips. I never did it again, and I was never asked again. I did enjoy distributing the poll cards around another voting area just before an election, and, towards the end of summer, taking around the electoral register forms. It was an easy area to cover as almost everyone returned the forms forthwith.

Yet some houses were a complete mystery. Whenever I called on one, behind its tall walls, there was no one ever in, no one ever came to the front door, though different cars stood in the drive, and it all seemed lived in. I found my way to front doors at the back of houses, to flats with their own entrance up fire escape stairs. I pushed forms into what seemed an inadequate post box, but that or nothing. I searched for secret flats, assured by other residents 'There's no such number'. One had a hidden staircase known only to the occupants, me and, hopefully, the postman. One basement flat was almost an underground bunker; only some unremarkable steps gave it away. Another flat turned out to be what I had taken as the house next door. It was renumbered later, I think.

I counted milk bottles on doorsteps to see if anything had changed since my previous visit. I came to know the people who were quite hopeless at returning the form until the last possible moment, but who would cheerily greet me, and/or tell me their life story, every time I called. I was so irritated when the lady of a well-built, well-maintained, detached house said, in a dismissive way, she never voted. My mother had to wait until she was 28 to vote, having been a teacher for seven years. Now 18-year-olds have the vote.

Elections in the Covid year of 2020 were cancelled and, come the elections of 2021, I was glad that I had kept the postal vote arrangement even though I had retired several years back from being a poll clerk, or from anything else to do with the process. And so, I read the instructions, signed this, sorted various ballot papers, put these in that, then all that in there. Job done! Having no other reason to go into town to hand my envelope with my precious ballot papers in at the town hall, even if that were possible, I posted it.

Come election day, I regretted that. I could have walked up to the hall and handed my envelope in there. It would have been interesting to see just how Covid security was managed. But the main reason for my regret was that I missed the sense of taking part in the democratic process, of physically being part of a community. The act of taking the vaccine earlier this year had had that meaning and importance. One was doing something not only for oneself but also for the community. And so, next year, I will opt out from the postal vote and return to walking across the park to cast my vote in the proper way.

39. A Warwick Walk

16 May 2021

No. of UK cases: 1,926
No. of estimated Worthing cases: 17

I am quite sympathetic with those who have no desire to leave home turf yetawhile, even though Covid cases seem to have fallen as low as they are ever likely to be. But perhaps I have a wide view of 'home turf'! So it was that from the comfort of my preferred seat again on the coach I was glad to see the lines of the wooded Surrey Hills and feel the sharp turn away from the M23, onto and uphill the M25. It had been nearly a year! It was lovely to see again old, familiar friends of the road – an Eddie Stobart truck sweeping by, the big trucks of the big superstores, a National Express coach, Parcel Force's big red trucks, the Oxford Bus Co.'s brightly coloured 'Tube' to London.

The watchtower of Heathrow Airport came into view and, yes, there was a plane to watch – one plane in an otherwise empty sky. Yet scarcely any of the big European haulage companies were on the road, though the service station was full of hauliers and a Covid testing station too for them. Some naughty truckers, in the absence of the touring holiday coaches, were taking their chance to park close by the café in the area designated for coaches. My Worthing Coach and one other coach were the only rightful occupants.

The coach came down off the Cotswold escarpment and memories of the Didcot Cooling Towers[53] returned. Their comforting 'teddy bear' shape had gone years back, but the last chimney, at 660ft one of the tallest structures in the UK, came down only in February 2020, just after my last journey this way. We swept past the Oxford turn off, and in due course entered Royal Leamington Spa. In warm May sunshine, it looked considerably better than when last seen, when I vowed never to visit again. That day two years back had started badly. The alarm had not gone off! When I did wake, I was left with 10 minutes to get myself up, dressed and into the car. I did it! I caught the coach and spent the rest of the day out of sorts, wondering why I had come, in sleet showers and cold rain, to this dreary town.

I was not here to stay on this occasion, but because the coach was moving on to Warwick, of which I had happy memories. Interesting houses in variety, half-timbered black-and-white-framed buildings jostled with handsome stone villas of colonnades, porticos and pediments. Wide streets, narrow alleys, and a market square with plenty of space for open-air living. Just the place to visit when you can eat only outdoors. And Warwick has a castle! That was where the coach had put us down on the previous trip, so it was disconcerting today when we drove past and stopped at the far end of town in the bus station. It put an extra 10 minutes on my plans for the day, there and back.

---

53 Didcot power stations, https://en.wikipedia.org/w/index.php?title=Didcot_power_stations&oldid=1054193590 (last visited 22 December 2021).

Plan A was to take advantage of the double destinations of the day and walk the riverside path from Warwick and pick up the coach in Leamington. Plan B was to do something different. Having looked at the map, OS. 221 'Coventry and Warwick', I realised that on the Warwick trip I had found the first part of the walk in St Nicholas Park and, on the Leamington trip, perchance had walked the last stretch through Victoria Park and into Jephson Gardens. It was the middle section I did not know and that looked the most interesting.

Noting a few waymarks, I hurried quickly through the town and into the formal Gardens of St Nicholas Park, dallied awhile at the café, and continued on through the children's play area. By this time the river was easing its way out of tidy Parks & Gardens borders and mown grass and had turned to meet my direct path near the elegant bow of the Charter footbridge. Crossing that was for later, hopefully. I followed the path, which led into a 1950s (or so) housing development but soon realised the best part of the houses was towards the river so, via a twitten, finally reached the footpath proper and the riverbank. This was more like a country walk, through long grass, between unkempt trees and ivy overgrowing stumps, though the gravel and cinder path showed it was well-used.

The path dipped under a low bridge just as a train conveniently thundered overhead to confirm this as the rail bridge. Shortly after, another, higher bridge appeared and, on its further side, a flight of steep metal steps. I clambered up these and looked around me. The Grand Union Canal[54] offered sunshine and tranquillity in both directions. Young

_____

54   Grand Union Canal, https://en.wikipedia.org/w/index.php?ti-tle=Grand_Union_Canal&oldid=1057094164 (last visited 22 December 2021).

goslings eager for the joyousness of spring raced ahead of their parents who, grumbling 'Don't … Be careful … Look where you're going', followed on. For possibly the first time ever, I looked over the edge of an aqueduct. Very odd to have disciplined, contained water behind me and yet to look down to the rough, untamed River Leam flowing eastwards.

It was so peaceful walking the canal. A low farm bridge humpbacked over it, giving barely enough headroom at the side. In the fields sheep slowly munched their way across the meadow. The occasional birdsong outlined the silence. I came to the signpost pointing the link across to Princes Drive. That, I hoped to return by in due course. For now, I passed over another trainline and came to the A425 and a built-up area. These were, surely, old industrial warehouses transformed into elegant flats with some new flats constructed in the same austere style. The canal flowed and wavered, presented me with a gate through to a big superstore – very handy for needy users of the path and canal. Perhaps even more welcome was the canalside pub. I was tempted to join a cheerful crowd of users on its outside patio but moved on to my turning point away from the canal.

The walk had taken less than an hour so far. All I had to do now was survive crossing two busy roads and a retail park, then find, among an industrial area, the Warwick-bound end of the link back to the canal. I walked down a noisy road between the Household Waste Disposal site on my left and a railway viaduct on my right and began to recognise where I was. This was as far as I had come on my unhappy visit to Leamington when I had unwittingly followed the riverside path. I was pleased to link up and even more so to see the signpost pointing me onto the return footpath.

Past the noisy tumbling weir, along the path cheered by a few last daffodils, yellow, white, single, double, I reached open heathland and some trees carrying deep red or white cherry blossom. A few moments later, I was among the sheep and back to the canal. The occasional narrowboat chugged past me; cyclists, walkers or runners shared the path as I walked back, and walked on past the metal steps, partly lured by the never-ending open canal before me, to pass under the A445 Emscote Road. The plan was that I should leave fairly soon after, assuming there would be access to the road from the towpath, which was not always the case.

Much relieved to see a metal rail on the side of the towpath, placed where it would stop anyone rushing down a path from falling into the canal, I turned into Charles Street, almost immediately into Wharf Street, then left through a pair of black 'gates' into a quiet, enclosed residential park. The central manicured lawns were for residents only and the big redwood trees that overshadowed them. I followed the silent path through the 'village', between old, distinguished housing and the new, keeping up the standard. Thus, on my left, I saw a sign to a joint cycle and foot path, heading back to Emscote Road. It offered certainty, whereas my first intention to continue rested on the hope for something similar later on. So, following it, I found myself shortly after back at the root of the Charter Bridge, but uncertain whether the original intention would have given a more enjoyable route.

The bridge took me (and lots of schoolkids) almost to different country the other side. Swelling land, rising and falling folds replaced the flat landscape I was used to. Large watery havens for wildlife spread to my left where a pair of white swans gathered. I headed homewards through a simple gate beyond the car park entrance into Myton Road. Over Castle Bridge the splendid view of Warwick Castle[55] and its sheer cliff face reflected into the river below halted me briefly, and so into town.

The round trip had taken about two hours, but, more than being pleased with the way it had worked out, I had made progress in easing out of lockdown. What I had needed was assurance that other people responded to Covid in much the same way as I and my friends did. In returning to familiar places by familiar means, the more confident I have become that the routine of fumbling with face masks as we enter and leave shops is widespread, that social distancing in queues is now a natural habit. We have all suffered the same long, hard grind of a Covid winter. Now the soft warm air of a lovely May day gave promise that the habits and skills acquired generally would enable us all to enjoy moving around more widely, more freely, yet safely.

---

55   Warwick Castle, https://www.warwick-castle.com.

May – Getting Somewhere

from 17 May 2021

Up to 6 people can meet indoors, or 2 households only. Hospitality can re-open indoors. Indoor group sports and exercise can re-open

Outdoor gatherings up to 30 can meet. The majority of the indoor and outdoor economy can reopen.

40. Back to Work!

26 May 2021

No. of UK cases: 3,180
No. of estimated Worthing cases: 12

That Monday morning feeling! Only times 50 or more. It's over a year since our little group of volunteers at High Salvington Windmill had switched off the heating and the lights, unsure of what was to come. I had returned a week later on 23 March to tidy up loose ends and to leave a note about what to do when we returned, expecting, as I recall, that that would have been in about three to four months. I hope that note does not seem too cryptic now!

We had kept in touch over the year, emailing fairly regularly though, at times, finding it difficult to recall anything of interest to report. And we had met from time to time for coffee, as the rules about meeting 'other households' came and went. We had, at one time last September, even contemplated returning to 'work', understanding the category we came under to be 'charitable work'. This was allowed in principle, we thought, though our 'work' was not by any means vital to the community or country, or even the maintenance of the project.

We marked out and named our work stations, sloshed sanitiser and anti-bac around, discussed work practices like wearing face masks, not looking straight at each other, wearing gloves when handling common items, the space needed for 'social distance'. We marked out routes to and fro on the floor … and … and decided it was all too difficult. We could *either* be fairly Covid safe and secure *or* be comfortable and at ease, but not both at the same time. So we went for comfort and retired to a garden for coffee (as allowed).

But this time would be for real. We would use our work stations as set out, keep face masks to hand should we need to gather closely for discussion purposes. Now it was better weather (in theory) we could have the door open, maybe have a fan going to improve airflow. Would that be enough? Would it seem over the top? How would our occasional visitors fit in?

'Absence makes the heart go fonder,' it is said.[56] It also gives time and space for reflection on our activities as a semi-autonomous unit within a bigger project. All the pluses and minuses of that relationship came to mind, also of one's own personal relationship and situation as a volunteer. Did one want to go back to the old times and ways? Did one want to go back at all?

And/or just meeting up with other people and their expectations. Did one still have those skills, those standards after 12 months of living in one's own comfortable old clothes? I mean that both literally and as a metaphor, for doing one's own thing in one's own way but now having to come back to accepted standards, to be proper and to do things properly.

---

56 https://quotes.yourdictionary.com/articles/who-said-absence-makes-the-heart-grow-fonder.html.

Maybe that wasn't the concern so much of the 'office', but it was in the back of my mind about going back to the studio for ballet.* I had been trying to keep up to standard and hopefully even improve a little by doing classes online, but certainly felt nervous about stepping back into the public world. My energy input was not as much online and at home as it was in real class. It was too easy to be distracted by a banging door, or just give oneself permission to feel a bit tired, a bit bored, not doing things real sharpish, not really meeting the challenge of making an effort.

I had indulged in all the opportunities there are at home for being a little sloppy, like at school playing around in the back row when you think teacher's not looking. What really kept me going and trying to make a routine and some effort was the thought that if I eased back too far or gave up altogether, I would never get going again. I kept on because I was keeping on.

I could just be grateful for the skill of our teacher to adapt dance movements and steps to the confined space in which we all were working, and to accompany them with a wonderful variety of music. A blessing of social media was also the feedback and posts of other onliners doing the same classes, having the same struggles at times, asking helpful questions, and sharing jokes, thoughts, photos, and news items.

The downside of technology is when it doesn't work. The most awkward occasion in my online career was when the picture froze but the sound – the music and instruction – continued. I struggled on listening to the sound, but then the picture went into fast forward mode to catch up while the sound continued at standard speed! Mind completely boggled, I switched off. Another day, another session!

I was also looking forward to starting Taiji again which seems to me to combine nicely slo-mo exercise with meditation practice! Having barely begun before Lockdown closed us down, I could not continue without guidance. I had found an online version, but not at a time or day convenient. So I was nervous about re-joining the group.

How did it work out first time round? What was in common, when we did meet and braved the cheer and challenge of other people's energy, was the pleasure that we all had in coming together again. Everyone was relaxed, happy, just glad to meet up with real people with a shared interest. To know we had survived. Anything else was secondary.

And so, for three days on the trot I got up smartish, put on smartish clothes and was in the due place at the due time. And home today; back to lockdown sloth? No, no, the whole world has changed. I'm home for the weekend – a four-day weekend. Sounds good!

*P.S. those who remember my early attempts at ballet, described in the first blog, may like to know of my progress. We are now putting steps together, as follows:

> *Galumph to the left. Pootle to the right!*
> Oh, again? Sorry!
> *Galumph to the left. Pootle to the right!*
> *Galumph to the left. Pootle to the right!*
> Oh, again, but the other way round?
> Very sorry!

41. Spring into Summer

2 June 2021

No. of UK cases: 4,330
No. of estimated Worthing cases: 10

The cordyline palms along Worthing promenade once more looked to have the right setting, with a blue sea behind them, blue skies over, and warm sunshine shadowing their spiky leaves on the pavement. Further along the seafront, encouraging smells came from the wood-burning pizza van, the burger van and the gooey cakes van. All announced that spring was here. And so were the customers, in their summer clothes. Already some had taken to the sun a little unwisely and their unshielded arms, unprepared for summer sun, were bearing the scorch marks.

'No Mow May' had happened from necessity as well as choice. When I did finally set the mower to work it was more like giving it a mud bath as it struggled with long wet grass. And the wind-withered leaves of the shrubs showed the effect of a cold, dry April. At long last, we could cast aside the winter duvets, turn off the heating finally, confident that the temperature would still extend its rise. Not even a Bank Holiday Monday would stop that.

And after two weeks 'back at work' it was nice to have a Bank Holiday. I was just getting into the rhythm of the week again and its new structure, but there is not going to be another holiday for three months. However, there are summer holidays to break up the next three months, assuming I get to booking some such, which I'm not too sure about yet. I'm more likely to go out on day trips and exercise my rights as a volunteer to ring up and say, 'Sorry, can't come in today.'

And so down to the town centre to enjoy the holiday and see what gives. And, wonderfully, lots. After the desolation of the Covid winter, it was a pleasure to walk among crowds or at least be in the company of other people in the shopping precincts, to see pubs with open doors and to hear from open windows the chink of glasses, the sound of happy voices, bursts of laughter, high-pitched giggles of excited children.

People still stood in shop entrances fumbling with masks. At some, a short queue awaited entry. Smaller shops in particular were still limiting numbers of customers. Most asked for people preferably to shop alone and gave guidance of one-way entrance and exits. All offered dollops of hand sanitisers – these varied in texture, from thick jelly-like ones to flowing liquid – and a paper towel to dry your hands on. Some shops, uncertain whether the dispensers were to be used on the way in or on the way out, had placed them ambivalently between, so were little used either way. Rather like the donkey who died of hunger because he was midway between two bales of hay and could not decide which to eat. I think I used the stuff more on the way out.

Families were walking the area leisurely, without the intensity of Christmas shopping, or even the urgency of the usual must get this, get that, and get home outing. It was a version of the Mediterranean walkabout, where seeing around is as important as being seen out, and to enjoy being out for its own sake. For which purpose, notably, the place to go is the Pier, passing by, of course, the beaches. These were nicely full of families, each with its own comfortable social distancing from the next, though we did that a long while before Covid required it. It seems as if, as soon as we sit down, we want space between us and them in a way we do not when standing up or moving around.

And people – adults – swimming in the sea! It was something around high tide, I imagine, when the beach and depth of seawater for swimming are near at hand. Get it wrong in Worthing and you can walk a long way with cold water still barely above your knees. An upright paddler was working his way around the pier over a fairly calm sea. Or that's how it seemed from the deck of the pier. Probably not so to him.

I was about to enter the Pier[57] when I realised I was stepping over *No Entry* signs stuck on the ground, and hurried to the other side of the dividing kiosk to make the appropriate entry. It was the shady, windy side, though the wind was gentle. The divider between the two sides, which I had always thought of as a windbreak more than anything, was a screen of glass panels.

In recent years, on the initiative of the *Worthing Journal*,[58] these panels have been commissioned by various institutions and organisations of the town to portray their

57 Worthing Pier, https://en.wikipedia.org/w/index.php?title=Worthing_Pier&oldid=1058889231 (last visited 22 December 2021).

58 Worthing Journal, http://worthingjournal.co.uk.

activities and contribution to the town. More recently, coloured glass panels have been added. Through these the sun now shone and coloured the decking.

I chose not to walk the length of the pier to the stage from which ships in the past have taken or unloaded passengers. Alternatively, get a really low tide and you may be able to walk around the pier altogether, though a weird combination of swimsuit and walking boots could be the safest attire. Nor did I enter the Southern Pavilion, restored a few years ago to its Streamline Moderne[59] 1930s splendour. Instead, I took my coffee to the sunny side of the pier and found a seat on a bench there.

Some years back, I had hosted for a weekend some Chinese students under a Foreign and Commonwealth Office initiative and had taken them on the Pier for a look around. They looked back at Worthing's seafront hotels and buildings and declared, 'it was the most beautiful town they had ever seen'. It was a day when the sea was an emerald green, the sky a royal blue and the seafront buildings in smart black-and-white attire. But even so…?

They were also entranced by being able to walk over the sea. I am, on the other hand, slightly uneasy about this. It goes back to my first childhood encounter with piers, Brighton Palace Pier in particular. During WW2, piers had, in general become no-go places, bound and gagged with barbed wire and more, and a large central hole blown in the middle to prevent the enemy landing.

So I was probably around 13 before I have any serious memory of going on the Pier, and I did not like it. I did not like the fact that you could see between the planks of

59   Streamline Moderne, https://en.wikipedia.org/w/index.php?title=Streamline_Moderne&oldid=1056174800 (last visited 22 December 2021).

the decking and see a lot of heaving water underneath. This experience I repeated when I first put on a snorkel years later in the warmth of the Mediterranean Sea, and put my head under the surface and saw all these waving plants around ready to grab me. Never again!

Today, the sea and its little wavelets were sparkling in the sun. Looking between the gaps between the planks, one could still see them glitter and twinkle. It was as if all the stars in the night sky were stored for the day under Worthing Pier!

A young couple made space for me on their bench, giving a certain amount of space between us but not one-metre-plus, for sure. A fisherman, tired of learning against the rail hopefully, looking for a nibble, retired to another. People walked by with or without coffee or ice creams, but the numbers decreased.

Time to go. Worthing seems flat enough along the coast but there is a slight steady incline as you walk inland, just enough to be off-putting. And, in any case, I needed a bit of shopping! With no great need for a disciplined shopping routine, I could drop in and get a couple of items just like the old days, then take the bus home.

42. Ticket to Ryde

12 June 2021

No. of UK cases: 7,738
No. of estimated Worthing cases: 34

Very gratifying to hear the train conductor say as he checked my ticket, 'My! That's a long journey.' My horizons had been diminishing as my inertia grew, so I had decided to make the effort and 'go beyond', or at least, take a journey requiring a change of trains. The trip itself would be the purpose of the day rather than to go somewhere, do a bit of sightseeing then to return home. Today there would be no return. All would be outward bound!

In a simple way, 'going beyond' from the south coast of England means going past Southampton, which is the great access point for, as it says on the M27, 'The West'. A vista of wonderful landscapes opens before the mind's eye with that evocative call, as also when, on Southampton Station, the names of exciting but unknown places are reeled out by the station announcer. I hope the feeling is reciprocated by those travelling west to east. This time, however, the announcement was that my onward train westward had been cancelled. Another was to hand, yet I was uneasy about a further connection.

The train had worked its way past Southampton port, had passed the multicoloured, multistacked pile of containers awaiting their onward journey, whichever way that was, inbound or outbound. There was no sign of the big cruise ships that had filled the skyline of the docks last autumn; maybe they are at last 'cruising'? Thus, I stood in the peace and quiet of Brockenhurst Junction, admiring the mauve rhododendrons and, in the steady breeze, the horse chestnuts gently waving their ice-cream cones of flowers. Then the last train of the morning wound its way past the yachts and boats and ships on the Lymington River and came to its resting place. It could go no further. From here on, I needed a ship. I must be going beyond!

I had booked online with Wightlink and printed out my ticket, but at the point of entry to the ship I was instructed to make the ticket available for scanning. No QR code or some such had been printed. I pointed this out to the man with the scanner and, from behind the face mask of another standing by, came: 'Speak the number.' Thus enlightened as to what QR is about, I boarded the ship. Another counted us in; clicked in, not clocked on.

From the open deck I watched the stately process of the ferry negotiate the twisting channel of the river. Out at last, the ship altered course slightly. Low cloud-cum-mist came and went but in the best moments we could see Hurst Castle guarding the entrance to the Solent and the stacks of the Needles beyond, in open water.

It had taken half the journey time to get out to sea, so it was not long before we closed in on Yarmouth, Isle of Wight. Not everyone's idea of 'going beyond' perhaps, but, with its green landscape certainly putting it on the green list, I caught the Needles Breezer bus. This took us at a serene and gentle pace down country lanes and between green fields nourishing sheep, corn, buttercups in plenty and meadows generally. The occasional commentary passed on useful information about the landscape: the geography, the history, the animals, the people. We passed thatched cottages with yellow sandstone walls, a thatched church; went through the narrow streets of Freshwater and to Alum Bay.[60]

The sun that had cheered our crossing was now hidden behind thick low cloud. Some brave holidaymakers, not too many for Covid safety but hopefully enough to encourage the providers, were making their way around the attractions, possibly to investigate the chairlift to the beach and a close-up view of the many shades of colours in the sandstone cliffs. The bus toiled its way up the steep road leading to the Old and New Battery stations at 400ft above sea levels, while the commentary continued on describing what now could not be seen because of the cloud. This, unfortunately, included the Needles themselves, though the colours of Alum Bay cliffs could be discerned as we returned below the cloud. It was both the high point and the low point of the day!

Seeing my next bus waiting, I took my chance and changed to service bus no. 7. Like all local buses, it heeded little as it sped towards Newport in and out the villages, passed red-bricked Victorian terraces that lined the route. Signs to bring sightseers to the Newtown Creek Nature Reserve, Carisbrooke Castle, Newport Roman Villa did not distract me. Nevertheless, I restrained myself from hopping forthwith onto the next onward bus, though it stood at its stop, ready to depart.

As one never knows for sure, when, or whether the next bus will arrive as per the timetable, I had taken all

60   Alum Bay, https://www.theneedles.co.uk/landmarks/alum-bay.

that came. As buses had turned up just as needed, the journey so far had been too easy for my own good. It was now quite a while since I had had a little something in the passenger's café at Lymington and looked out over broad stretches of water intermingled with grassy knolls. Cream tea in the nearest café would also be a nod to the sightseeing. I also had the comforting knowledge that the onward bus service had a high frequency! More hand sanitiser to slosh on. They seemed everywhere today, on stations, in cafés, on buses. More Test and Trace forms to fill in.

Out of Newport in its rush hour, the bus struggled along narrow Victorian roads not built for large cars in quantity, and between more red-brick houses packed in between the fold of hills and river. It stopped briefly to pick up and put down passengers as required. Past the top end of Fishbourne Creek, Quarr Abbey[61] was signed, and so into the fine houses at the top of Ryde hills, stylish 18th– to 19th-century buildings with stone facades. The strong breeze had at last blown the clouds away, the sun was out, and I could now see across the blue water to the mainland and the landmark of Portsmouth's Spinnaker Tower[62] and, at sea, the Spithead Forts.[63]

I walked the few steps along the Esplanade to the Hoverport.[64] Within a few minutes the hovercraft drew itself up from the water and floated over the foreshore to settle down close by. It was uncanny. Boats can't do that. Cars can't do that. I've been on a hydrofoil and that didn't do that either. Planes have to work very hard to travel in

61   Quarr Abbey, https://quarrabbey.org
62   Spinnaker Tower, https://www.spinnakertower.co.uk.
63   Spithead Forts, https://friendsofstokesbay.co.uk/spithead-forts.
64   Hovertravel, https://hovertravel.co.uk

two mediums. It was something a sea monster would do, only this was like the movement of a nesting bird and, similarly, was comfortably rounded and friendly, and quiet. While the engines are noisy there's no grinding or bumping sound from the hull – it is friction-free.

We passengers walked in. On board, I walked to the back of the cabin and took the inner seat of a double. The tactic worked: no one pushed past me to take the outer window seat. The hull rose to the level of the black rubber curtains, and we were off. Whether we were over land, shallows or deep water was immaterial: we moved at a car's speed. The breeze was giving the yachts a good sail and the black rubber bounced around a bit. Then into the hard at Southsea. The hovercraft nestled down, and we walked out.

One more easy transfer to the waiting bus, the rail station and another train. Somewhere out of Portsmouth the line merged with the main east–west coastal line, and at the first station thereafter I boarded the final train of the day. I'd done the round. I was, I now had to admit, homeward bound.

The reward was to have a cold beer in the garden: almost my first moment of fresh air of the day. It had been a remarkably inside and sedentary day, while everybody else did the work. And I could take off my face mask, for sure. It had been very nearly possible to divest myself of it on the first train outward when, for one moment, I thought I was going to have the coach to myself. But another came on board, leaving empty only 60 seats! Thereafter, there had been a comfortable number of people around.

On the last leg of the day the train had seemed busy. Travellers were either getting home for the day or going out for a Friday evening jolly. Only then was I aware of face masks not being worn as expected. Two young men came on carrying phones, cans and face masks. The cans and phones were put to the appropriate parts of their faces, but the face masks remained in their hands. Use of a face mask seemed to contradict their lifestyle, as I had observed on a local bus during the week when a mother and teenage daughter had gotten on, fashionably dressed and beautifully made up, but no face mask to ruin the effect.

But I had been in an ambivalent situation on the Needles Breezer. I had taken an upstairs front seat (of course) and on the opposite front seat and the seat behind was a party of three or four, chatting among themselves and not, I now recall, wearing face masks. I wasn't bothered. It didn't seem like a bus. While the rear half was open to all weathers, the front part of the upper deck was closed off to give, thankfully, protection against the English summer. It was like being inside where the 'not more than 6' rule applied.

The day had not been one of true going abroad travel, but it had required going beyond the usual routes and the home zone, and gave me a feel of achievement and satisfaction. Last August, when I wrote the two-part blog 'Day Tripper' (Blogs 14 and 15), I had had in mind some follow-up. I had not expected it to take so long before this 'Part 3' would be written.

June – Hold-Up!

The original roadmap had envisaged that all legal restrictions would end on 19 June but, with Covid numbers high, this was delayed until 19 July.

43. Extra Time

21 June 2021

No. of new UK cases: 10,633
No. of estimated Worthing cases: 125

There are several ways of 'going out', I've realised, and it is not always necessary to go for the Big Day Out, as last week. The weather being cold, wet and windy, it was sufficient to go to a superstore across town that I had not been to since Christmas. On my way I stopped for petrol and was shocked to see the price. I don't think I have paid that much ever before, and so much higher than it fell to in lockdown, when not a car moved.[65] Traffic these days is pretty well back to normal, pre-Covid levels.

Then, for the first time for months, I did not turn right at the traffic-lights but kept straight on into almost 'unknown' certainly 'forgotten' territory, though I almost needed to give myself special permission to do so. Familiar yet unfamiliar landmarks popped up before me like jack-in-the-boxes. Muscle memory turned the car into the right position for awkward corners. The car remembered where

---

65   RAC Foundation, https://www.racfoundation.org/data/uk-pump-prices-over-time. Petrol prices: 29 May 2020 = 106.83; 18 June 2021 = 130.87p per litre.

the junctions were and slowed accordingly. Nothing had changed except the amount of traffic coming in from here, coming along from there. Had I just forgotten the time and the routine of picking up the children from school and it was that filling the roads? Was there some hold-up somewhere and the usual alternatives were being used? Some people, I think, prefer travel by private car as a form of security from Covid; others, as I am today and as ever, for the convenience it gives.

Big shops have changed and adapted their Covid security as time has moved on. Separate entrance and exits have been formalised where previously it was either or both. Very rarely now do you see a guardian at the door counting people in. At some shops a traffic light system is used; others seem more relaxed altogether about numbers. But almost always, nowadays at the entrance there is a table where a range of sanitisers stands ready. I preferred the spray kind until I read the notice saying, 'Don't use on your hands'. It is for trolleys and basket handles! So far, no problem. My hands are still here.

And there are more screens around guarding the cashiers from the customer, though at times they inconvenience both. More self-operating tills are available too, sometimes with a staff member hovering around to explain the system or sanitise it after each customer's use. Most usefully they come to sort out problems, when you can't get the barcode to register because the number or package has been squashed, or because you have been too slow in putting it in the right place, or because a human has to check you are over 21. Oh yes, I am, by a long way! They ought to be able to do that by remote by now. I have even mastered two of the pay-at-the-pump systems hereabouts!

Some shops still have big arrows on the floor hoping their customers will shop in a well-organised way. Other stores have realised the impossibility of that. I do have my own route and routine and I do go around the shop in a fairly well directed manner, but I'm sure it's my own, not general. And, of course, while I go directly from buying this here to getting that there, on the way will detour to see what they have in over in that aisle! Whatever direction the arrow points, if the way is clear I nip down. We are not going to be taken off our route and routine just by Covid!

I went shopping with a friend once who had quite a different diet and quite different tastes from mine. That trip took me to shopping aisles I didn't know existed and to foods I had no idea what to do with. This is why, from time to time, supermarkets change everything around to make us go down aisles we avoid just to see different goodies, as a shop assistant told me when I asked why it happened – and, he added, it also foils shoplifters. They find the best route out and changing the position of whatever makes a quick getaway more difficult.

None of these changes is required by law. They are not mandatory upon us or the shops in the way that face masks are. They come under the guidance 'hands, face, space'. And we can choose whether we will so act and to what extent, as in 'you can take a horse to the water, but you can't make it drink'. It comes from our own reading of the situation and our own degree of caution and care and concern. And, although we are now into extra time for the rules and mandatory requirements, with some assurance that that is for another month only, it seems to me open whether the guidance will remain recommended practice as our role as part of UK Team Vaccine versus the Virus Squad continues.

The rain continued to fall heavily but unsteadily. At least the car was getting a much-needed organic cleaning as I headed for the Household Waste Disposal Site, to give it its full title. And I had with me the paperwork required, the booking confirmation and reference number, and my identification papers. I had been warned by a neighbour about an earlier visit, when the queue stretched nearly half a mile down toward the main road and people who had booked were being outplayed by people who had not; everyone was out of time and out of order.

I came ever closer with no other car in sight and drove alongside the little stream, the Teville. It is always a pleasure to be there, partly because it encourages one when in the queue that one is closing in on the actual site, and secondly because its green banks and wild flowers in season cheer the surrounding industrial landscape. At the gate, still no cars, and certainly no attendant to check the paperwork. It was so empty still and silent, I doubted momentarily that it was open.

I stopped to put a bag of textiles into the maw of one of the cabinets: like feeding the lions, or maybe crocodiles? Usually, I take them to one managed by a charity, but there was nothing in here shopworthy, and it made one trip out of it. This requires a bit of a detour from the main passage and negotiating one's way back into the mainstream depends on the kindness of a car driver to give way. No problem today, so up the ramp to the final frontier. Here one may also need to negotiate with a car in the adjoining stream to agree who moves first. Occasionally an attendant acts as a kind of DJ and calls one in and points out a vacant slot.

No attendant today and amazingly more empty bays than cars, partly, I then thought, because of the requirement to use alternate bays. I took my first load along to the 'catchall' bay – household waste. Usually there is a group of helpful attendants around who take the awkward stuff from me to the right bay. Not today, not in Covid times but this was small stuff. But I needed direction and found an attendant in a yellow high-vis jacket sheltering under a large umbrella. From behind his face mask he pointed out the bin for the batteries. Others asked him – some wearing face masks, others not – what to do with this, where to put that. In a friendly way, he explained.

I discussed with a driver in the next (socially distant) bay the merits of booking and our allowance of visits. Then we each took off our sodden face masks, and went our separate ways home.

44. Bon Appetit!

26 June 2021

No. of new UK cases: 18,270
No. of estimated Worthing cases: 170

The smell of freshly baked bread lured me through the doorway. I stood in a medium-sized tearoom, an adjunct to an artisan bakery, and of the kind I call 'designer rustic' – long scrubbed tables, some with bench seats, some with heavy individual chairs. The interesting menu was skilfully done to look artless, and as if written in chalk on a blackboard. Very likely the food and drink would be served in heavy pottery, but, unfortunately, the place had closed after the lunch service. No doubt they needed a break before beginning the bread-making shift.

I walked further up the narrow alley and through a gaggle of decaying buildings that opened onto a stream. Beside this was just enough room for a few tables and chairs to be set out. I took my seat at one of them, a metal table of vintage 1930 Parks & Gardens type, the chair made comfortable by a plump cushion. From one of the buildings the proprietress appeared and, in due course, served me with tea from a lovely china teapot, the style of which bore no relation to the other crockery on the table. It was all good china, lovely colours, lovely patterns, but nothing matched. This, for me, is the hallmark of the 'shabby chic' style.

Pubs create atmosphere differently. There is the genuinely old building in which the years have brought about different levels of floors, rooms reshaped, interesting inglenooks, cute corners. Or pub landlords may take over and adapt a building with its own history or style, such as a classic cinema with sweeping staircase and gilded balustrade, and create a decor to suit. Lacking these, pubs try to create character by making a purpose-built structure look 'olde worlde', with wooden beams and trusses here and there, place chimney breasts to divide a barren space with fires that look convincing only and create intimate areas out of settles – backboards for the seating or, contrariwise, put in low settees and even lower tables. One of the contradictions about eating out, especially when we're eating in, is that we want other people around, but want to be private too.

But with the advent of Covid, some niceties have returned. For a start you are likely to be shown to your table, to avoid tables that disturb social distancing requirements; especially if you have pre-booked, as for a group. And so, limited as we are for the time being to the size of the group, six is a good number to have at a table, preferably round. A round table is nothing like so spatially efficient as a rectangular table, but you can talk across that width as well as to one's immediate neighbours. Seated at a rectangular table, the diagonally opposite ends are too far to talk easily with, especially if you have hearing problems.

Even so, the table may well look a bit bleak for, having done their best to give the establishment as a whole some character and atmosphere, the detail is strictly functional and minimalist. No tablecloths, for a start, and probably no placemats. Neither is needed when the table, however wood-like, is man-made. The benefit this brings in Covid times is that a 'plastic' table surface (or oilcloth in some cases) is easily sprayed with sanitiser.

And probably no place setting of cutlery glinting silver-like on the bare table, as it might if set out in classic style. More often, and more Covid-secure, it is handed to you wrapped in a paper serviette as the meal arrives. No laundry bills to pay for heavyweight cloth napkins, but these were usually large, not the small skimpy pieces of paper that slip everywhere and stay nowhere.

But I can be sure I am not going to be embarrassed by a superabundance of cutlery as a place setting these days. Most eateries hand out just the basic pairing – knife and fork. If you choose a dessert, they do give you a spoon then, but one size fits all; no dessert fork, no round soup spoon rather than oval, no smaller knife for the bread roll (if any). Stainless steel was once the smart thing for cutlery to be made from, but now it is basic, functional, and will go through the dishwasher. Very rarely, I have been given a piece of stainless-steel cutlery heavy with decoration in a traditional silverware pattern. Its weight is a welcome feel in the hand.

This gives opportunity for the 'shabby chic' eatery, however! They may hand out a random collection of knives and forks, matching or not, but that may include cutlery with bone handles. Do bone handles survive the dishwasher treatment in a way that old wooden handles do not? Does this indicate that the establishment does not use dishwashers? Dishwashers are also inimical to cafetières, I've been told, which is another reason why we coffee drinkers have to watch our tea-glugging mates pour out cup after cup, whereas we coffeeholics are issued with one cup only, and charged extra for it! You may be given a steak knife with a wooden handle rivetted in some way, I think, to a serrated blade, as your dish is served. That, I find a little ominous! Is the meat really going to need a saw to cut through, or does it just indicate the limits of the standard stainless-steel blade?

The onset of Covid has also brought the return of table service. It makes the occasion seem so much more gracious if the waiter takes the order rather than battling at the bar, queueing at the counter, or tapping the app. Yet it seems unbalanced – maybe I'm out of practice – having a masked waiter to stand by my side, while I sit freely. Although I'm doing the talking and he/she the listening, it seems advisable to use sign language and point to the item you want on the menu, rather than rely on speech alone. And, as I read all the superlatives in the hyped-up description of what wondrous feast they offer, I wonder, or hope, have they paid the chef as much as they paid the copywriter?

Also, with everyone in the group speaking to the waiter you hear other's choices, which may bring about a change of plan as they mention something you had not spotted. Or, when the dishes appear, it is interesting to see what other people have chosen – and you can think, 'Glad I didn't choose that' – or have regrets when something you had dismissed appears, looking delicious and enticing. It's part of being a group, being the same but doing different.

And what we want to hear is the sound of people laughing and talking cheerfully. We have not had that for months. The world has been full of music and talk right enough, but canned. We may have spoken often enough to friends, but on the phone. What we have been deprived of is live sound. We may also have seen friends on Zoom, but you don't get from a screen that third dimension, the space and depth that physical presence gives. It is not just seeing and hearing and talking but actual being with is the delight. I am not a great one for hugging. It was not part of my family's way of doing things. I am happy just to sit indoors in a café around a table and talk to people for real and feel the warm vitality. The establishment can do its best to give us a good setting and a good start but it's us being sociable that brings it to life.

45. Against Nature?

8 July 2021

No. of UK cases: 32,551
No. of estimated Worthing cases: 240

Why is Nature supposed to be so good for us? I mused. I was sitting in the outside 'balcony' at the RSPB Pulborough Brooks Reserve,[66] looking at the wide scene below me. The pond close to hand, the wetlands beyond, the river banks across that and further away low hills. And surely there was yet a further line of hills? Indeed, to enclose our more modest uplands called Downs (as in dunes), the mist and low cloud had combined to produce a majestic range of dark shadowy mountains.

The calls of a few energetic birds disturbed the siesta of their fellows and, indeed, of the whole scene. No grazing cattle, no ambling sheep, no keen-eyed bird watchers either. Is it that, the stillness, the silence, that is so beneficial? But we had a lot of that in lockdown. It was certainly a spacious scene before me, and more or less one colour, green. Yet in our gardens we grow flowers in a variety of colours. There is enough variety in the greens of nature not to be monotonous, shades of green now that the trees and hedges are in full summer leaf. Sunlight gives shadows, and contrast

---

66 RSPB, https://www.rspb.org.uk/reserves-and-events/reserves-a-z/
    pulborough-brooks.

and shape and definition but today there was no sun. The air was warm and humid, yet there had been so much rain recently that as you brushed by the leaves the air changed to cold wet. Cumulatively, all the senses were pleased and delighted. Was that why I felt better for being there?

My mind had switched off. I am never quite sure what I want to do when I'm in the natural world. Should I sit and meditate? If you are going to close your eyes, why not stay home? At first, I am content to sit and look and enjoy being out in it all, but then I start to feel restless and start to amble around and look about me. But then it all seems pointless. Eye-stretching space is fine while you feel safe and in control. Lose your track in a wood and it stops feeling friendly.

Or was my dilemma only because I did not know what I was looking at in the way a naturalist would understand the scene, or a farmer, or a landscape historian? Is this a natural scene or as man-made as the town I had left behind me? Is it only a townie would think the scene natural? Or should I just make use of the scene, use the natural world as my gymnasium, and with a mountain bike rush up and down minimal tracks, bouncing off the potholes, ruts, roots and rocks?

My solution is to go for a walk. Should I go for a brisk walk? But if that means just walking up and down, there and back, that's not a walk, that's just exercise. Should I count the steps? Worse still. That reduces walking into function and technique, and a not human activity.

What's the difference? What makes a walk a human activity? A walk is making up a story and writing it with your legs. It has a beginning, middle and end. Not just getting there but getting back again. It uses the incidents of the natural world as its characters and weaves them together, puts them in relationship and gives you the problem of doing so and getting home again.

Nature seems tranquil only at the large-scale level I'm looking at. In detail, life is going on there with as much energy as possible. Maybe that's its trick. Maybe it is time that nature represents or, rather, timelessness. It's taken 10,000 years or so to bring about this landscape, umpteen generations of people and animals (big and little), and weather. Each negotiating with the other for its bit of space and time to make its life.

And the bit of nature that is affecting us mostly in our space and time is Covid-19. At least in this plague we know what is going on, as was not the case in previous ones. To some extent, 'Spanish' flu was understood but in previous plagues and pandemics sufferers had little idea or no idea what was happening to them and nothing more than common sense, to how to deal with it. And it seems that now we too are back to our common sense as lockdown ends shortly.

Suddenly, lockdown seems desirable. We know where we are with it. The rules and the guidelines, the security and reassurance it has given us. We want to wear masks. We want to keep to social distancing. People we don't know have had to obey and live in the same sort of way that we have. Will they now turn out to be a wild Covid-happy, mask-slinging marauding crowd? Or only the people, the usual suspects, who never took much notice at any time? But if we are all worrying about it, if the same concerns are widely shared, then we may continue to behave as we have done because everyone else is too. This has, to some extent, been the case all along.

I put down my empty cardboard mug. The café here was still operating on a takeaway service only basis. Maybe next time I come, when the winter birds are back, the cafetières will come out again and service will be inside. Let's hope.

46. Dancing in the 'Garden'

10 July 2021

No. of UK cases: 32,367
No. of estimated Worthing cases: 353

Breakfast is a personal meal and for me, preferably a solitary coming back to life slowly event. When it comes to one's own personal celebration, breakfast out is the ideal way to do so. So it happened that I was sitting in a restaurant in London's Victoria Station ready to celebrate my almost nearly final adventure in lockdown, and for braving the big city. Unfortunately, my favourite dish of Eggs Benedict was off, so I settled for a smallish big breakfast and, while waiting for my order to be served, had time to look around.

How much more pleasant travel is when there are not too many people around! I had been nervous about this journey, but the train was barely a quarter full. The platforms at Gatwick Airport were nearly as empty as they had been on my trip last August, as only the North Terminal was operating. More planes were parked around the terminal building than people inside, seemingly! How pleasant Victoria Station is when there are fewer people around. Enough to make it feel alive, but still enough space between to see the big patterning on the floor, and empty spaces on the big horseshoe sofas for which there was now enough room. How pleasant the inside of the restaurant was, as I walked through, with each table separated by a glass screen from its neighbour. This was a good time to travel before the world opened up (if it does) on 19 July and was the culmination of my various adventures out and around.

The app and the QR code had worked (another little triumph) so breakfast was duly served and enjoyed, and I walked out of Victoria Station pleased with myself. I was still nervous about travelling in the confines of the Tube, and not keen on the bus either. But what extraordinary buildings had gone up since I was last this way. *Take a length of steel and fold it over, then fill up the space in between with glass* seemed the principle, or *see how far you can push the centre of gravity and still keep the building upright* was another. The old blocks of dreary flats on the route into Victoria had been cheered by colourful cladding, making them a better companion for neighbouring Victorian red-and-white-striped brickwork; just hope the workmanship was as sound. I walked through a steel-and-glass arcade and came out into the quiet elegance of London houses, whose rectangular classic proportions gently upstaged the modern clever stuff.

Through Queen Anne's Gate into St James's Park, its status as a royal park marked by bronze crowns on the lampposts at either end of the bridge across the lake. Black coots with white foreheads were seemingly teaching their black chicks with red foreheads how to eat algae. One had gone aground in it and would have to eat his way out, or walk over the top. The brown furry heads of the small pochard ducks contrasted with the shiny greens and blues of the mallards. Big white swans and their mottled offspring kept their distance. And further along, a group of pelicans splashed around, their unwieldy big wings folded down, as angular as any mobile crane waiting for lift-off.

Camera-happy tourists gathered by a group of trees in which green parakeets were making their presence known while sombre, black-suited city pigeons huddled with hunched shoulders, disapproving of the noise. The big green trees in full leaf had seen it all before and their calming presence brought tranquillity. But had they seen elephants before? A small herd of them on the open grass was heading towards the neatly paired but fortunately empty deckchairs that lay in their path. Relax! The exotic life of St James's Park does not stretch so far. These were artwork elephants, made from a kind of cane by the villagers of southern India. The 'Elephant Family',[67] in total about one hundred, have been brought to UK by the charity Co-existence[68] as an example of how animals and humans can interact and co-exist.

I walked out the park and around by the National Gallery in Trafalgar Square. The main part of the square was closed off for big screen showing of the Euro 2020 finals. Singing made me think some fans had arrived a day too soon, but it was cheery singing by a group of gospel singers in equally cheery costume.

Up St Martin's Lane, the lights were on in the foyer of some of the theatres, but others were dark, closed. I turned into Floral Street. It leads appropriately towards Covent Garden and was alive with colour though not flowers. On either side of its length smallish bollards were placed at 10ft (or so) intervals, each bollard divided into sections of shafts and ring mouldings, with a bull's eye cap; seven

---

67   Elephant Family https://elephant-family.org.
68   Co-existence. https://coexistence.org.

sections in all and each a different bold colour and each bollard a different selection of colours! Leading from the Royal Ballet School gracefully over Floral Street was the concertina-like 'Bridge of Aspiration'[69] into the Royal Opera House itself. I too had my hopes set high!

For the first time, I was beginning to feel crowded and was wondering if I would join those who already had their face masks in position, a decision we shall face more often in the coming weeks, no doubt. And so, into Covent Garden Piazza where The Royal Opera House had taken to the streets with a pop-up summer festival 'ROH Unlocked'.[70] A long, low platform had been set up under a marquee roofing, and from this dais an ROH singer was teaching a group to sing a few notes of opera together with the appropriate actions while the crowd in festive mood looked on.

Then the dancers came on stage, bringing with them barres to hold on to. But the barres were intended for the public, and participants were invited. I had intended just to watch the first time around and then to decide whether to join or not. But maybe there was not to be a second chance. It was now or never! What had I to lose? No one there knew me! What did it matter? It wasn't a job interview and, in any case, I had failed plenty of those in the past and survived.

I stepped forwards, put on my face mask, sloshed the hand sanitiser around and with others took my place at one of the barres. Hands and arms to the left, legs and feet

---

69   Royal Ballet School, https://en.wikipedia.org/w/index.php?title=Royal_Ballet_School&oldid=1041689980 (last visited 27 December 2021).

70   Royal Opera House, https://www.roh.org.uk/tickets-and-events/festival/roh-unlocked-details.

to the right. Without a qualm, I did my version of what I thought was asked. It culminated in standing on tippy-toes, hands in graceful arc above (I hope) and then raising left knee out akimbo. Hold! Or not? But I did! for a few mini-seconds before gravity took over.

I returned to the crowd while the brass band section of the ROH orchestra played opera tunes and pop songs. But I was pleased with myself. Dancing with the Royal Ballet (to overstate wildly) was not something I could have done at all, was not even thinking of before lockdown. I shall enjoy Live Screenings from ROH at the cinema even more this coming winter. I took off my face mask. One feels the need to wear a mask when with people you don't know, but sharing a common interest creates that family feeling. And it was outdoors.

I needed a drink and possibly a little something as a reward. The myriad of cafés in the narrow streets had pulled out every table they could onto the pavement. All were filled now with happy people chatting away and all so exotic, Mexican, Japanese, Vietnamese, Korean, a far cry from the time when *spag. bol.* was the height of sophistication. So many, so crowded, I did not know which to choose and walked away.

I found a kiosk and took my tea into St James's Park again. The length of the lake one way had Buckingham Palace as background. Looking the other way, Nelson on his Column was framed by the trees and flowers, red begonias, orange and chocolate rudbeckia, blue convolvulus, purple loosestrife.

Then I saw the sign pointing to the ladies'. Undoubtedly the royal parks would charge. Would it be a 'pay by mobile' system? They, surely, would have the wherewithal to install that if anyone did. As ever, 20p was needed. I turned my bag upside down in the hope that lurking in the bottom would be the right amount in the right coinage. And then I saw the gadget and the sign, 'pay by card'! Pay 20p by contactless card? Well, I did. I shall have a souvenir of my visit to London on my bank statement.

Mission accomplished. I had braved the perils of a visit to London, though I shan't know for another week whether there has been any downside, and been encouraged to keep working away at Silver Swans[71] ballet. This was an almost final frontier on the return to normality. But had I stayed well because so many people had stayed home? Is it now my turn to stay in if other people begin to come out? I'm thinking to stay home a little while to see what happens.

---

71 Royal Academy of Dance, https://www.royalacademyofdance.org/dance-with-us/silverswans.

47. End in Sight

18 July 2021

No. of new UK cases: 48,161
No. of estimated Worthing cases: 586

Only coaches were filling the coach bays at the service station near Southampton, and our Worthing Coach took the last slot. The coach was full, every seat taken. Then a long queue at the ladies'. Normal service has resumed? Not quite. We were all wearing face masks, and our temperature had been taken at the wrist, (easier than at the forehead) as we boarded. Designated entrances took us into the service station, which was busy but not overly so, and arrows on the floor guided people around. It made dodging people so much easier as they looked for empty tables and seats while carrying unbalanced trays of food and hot drinks. By and large people were wearing face masks.

The rain had, so far, held off. Under the greyscale palette the sky was using, from grubby white to dirty grey, we passed ripening, yellow-gold fields outlined by summer dark green hedges. But dabs of white and flakes of pale blue came into play. To the north, some bright white clouds appeared as if out from a better wash cycle than the ones overhead.

While London traffic varies between lockdown and gridlock, country roads, if one may call the A35 that, can be bedevilled with tractors and the like. Today's traffic was grindingly slow, so we rolled onto the Esplanade at Seaton, East Devon, an hour later than planned. Wet pavements showed there had been rain around but none at this moment. Leaving the seafront, and the cliffs either side of the long Pebble Beach (is that special? it's standard at Worthing), I headed for the Seaton Tramway.[72]

Social distancing at the modern terminus was well enforced as we were allocated our seats and told we could not move whatever the weather. I took my chance with the open top deck and clambered up the steep winding stairs. One side of the top filled with passengers but social distancing prevented anyone sitting on the other.

The bell rang, brass levers clattered, metal wheels clanked on metal tracks, but no engine sound. That's what electric does or does not. We were off and up the estuary of the River Axe. Shorn sheep in green fields stared at us, birds on the wetlands – heron? avocet? – took no notice. On the other side of the river, the town of Axemouth relaxed in its afternoon siesta.

Before us, and between the green jungle an English summer creates, stretched the single track. Shock! Horror! Towards us came, in its wobbly way, another tram. We met at a passing place. Our driver stepped from his open cab and put in his baton at the red light. The points changed. The light became white. We danced around each other in a heavy-footed way and continued on.

The excitement of the trip was at Colyford Road Junction. Again, the driver worked the system. Lights came on, bells and hooters sounded, and we clanked

72 Seaton Tramway, https://www.tram.co.uk.

forward and across the open crossing. Through the wide valley of the Axe we trundled on and past Colyton Station to the end point. Trams are double headed so do not need a turning circle. The driver walked from one end of the tram to the other and swung the arm accordingly. Seeing this happen brought back childhood memories of trolleybuses in Brighton.

There was no time, sadly, to take the half-mile river walk into the town of Colyton itself. Rather, I headed for the station restaurant, to enjoy a late lunch of pork pie and salad, with a big pot of tea in matching white crockery; no 'shabby chic', no small stainless-steel teapot and no throwaway cardboard mug, thankfully. But where to partake? I could celebrate 'inside hospitality' by eating in the conservatory or, be served outside at one of the tables set out along the platform, amid the relaxation of the countryside, the interest of the trams and the hum of conversation from happy people. The niceties of post-Covid life have returned!

Something was bothering me. There was something odd going on. Something was not quite right. In some way I felt out of place. And that something, I realised, was Me. I was too big for the trams. We were all too big for the trams. And that's the fun of it. I was on a tram about two-thirds the standard size, as the driver confirmed. It is like adults playing with the children's toys, though all the serious stuff, as I had seen, was taken seriously and done properly. Enjoy!

I moved to the barrier for the next tram, but social distancing limited numbers so was denied the first in. One passenger was rather put out as he had left his car in a timed car park on the seafront. But no problem for me. I had allowed for this as I did not want to commit the sin of Being Late Back to the Coach, particularly so after the difficult outward journey. Indeed, a little walk around the town, along the seafront and into a hillside garden, assured me of the need for another visit, another time.

Back in Worthing I stepped off the coach aware of how great a pleasure it was to have been back on board, to have had another good day out away from the confines of living between coast and Downs, to have visited a 'tourist attraction' for the first time in a couple of years, and had the pleasure shared with others. I was grateful to all, and especially to Worthing Coaches who made these trips possible.

Thankfully, I took off the mask. Never to wear again? Back in May, when UK cases were down to about 1,650 and estimated Worthing cases about a dozen, it looked as if lockdown was coming to a triumphal end in June/July. Something clear cut and obvious, 'The End'. But it hasn't turned out that way. Next week we are off the tramlines of mandatory rules. We have done our time with the rules of the road. Only guidelines, 'arrows on the floor' will remain to bring some order to the infinitely chaotic movement of pedestrians around the space they use. But perhaps wearing face masks will not seem such a drag if we have a choice and can choose, voluntarily, when to wear them according to our own judgement.

July – We Think It's All Over?

from 19 July 2021

After the postponement from 21 June 2021, all legal limits on social contact are lifted.

All remaining businesses can reopen.

48. Back in Business

17 August 2021

No. of new UK cases: 26,852
No. of estimated Worthing cases: 886

A month after 'Freedom Day', with Covid numbers generally down in an unstable way, cafés are still asking for Test and Trace details. Or at least some are. The ones that did in lockdown. Table service by masked staff continues with some, but at the pub in Brighton, where my Oddfellows[73] lunch club recently reconvened after 18 months, no one was wearing masks. In the happily busy restaurant, bar staff were shielded by screens at the till. Other screens separated and shielded tables too close to the bar walkway. Sadly, table service was no more. I had to queue, but it was a small, definite queue, not the usual bar scrum.

I had been quite excited to be back on the bus going into Brighton. The group was not our usual full house of a dozen or more but over the meal re-establishing familiarity we managed to sort out, as we chatted, why snails climb up plastic doors, what second clarinettists do, face masks for singers, the rights and wrongs of grouse-shooting and the ID and vaccine passes required for football fans. How

---

73   Manchester Unity of Oddfellows, https://www.oddfellows.co.uk.

have I managed without such problem-solving discussions these last 18 months? But it takes a bit of getting used to again, the presence of people, the weight of personalities, and how the group fits together, and I found I had rather lost the knack and tired easily.

A picnic in the park for another group, for the same sort of reason, seemed a good idea, until the weather turned nasty. We had all been asked to bring our own food, but our instinct for personal space kicked in and we sat too far away from each other. The sense of sharing and being together that we all desired was lost. It became too formal, especially as our voices were wind-blown away by the ever-increasing strength of the onshore gale, and under the ever-growing shadow of rain that finally burst upon us.

It is a level of sociability that we have missed but which is now returning. This, the ordinary level somewhere in between having friends and family around in the garden or the house, and big commercial events and organisations. It is the level at which local societies and clubs that are not part of a big league operate. It is the kind of group that every town and village has: its art and photographic clubs, social groups, walking groups, heritage groups sustained by volunteers. The sort of small group that does not own its own space but hires rooms here or halls there. They have to find their way between getting functions for their members up and running on the one hand and, on the other, the Covid security arrangements that the government 'expects and recommends' venues to provide or require.

Event organisers are still asking their would-be participants to book. It may be because numbers at the venue are limited, and/or because the organisation is working the Test and Trace system themselves. I've been asked to sort out the wording for a form for an organisation's meeting. They have not asked members to book but, as the hall they are hiring from has asked for Test and Trace info, attenders will have to sign in when they arrive. Alternately, they may use their app, and zap the NHS QR code if the venue displays it. I am getting pretty good at zapping the QR code but usually have to wait so long for the phone to warm up that it's quicker to write in name and number.

Also, the venue may require face masks to be worn, seating may be controlled and sanitising afterwards required. Hirers may not use the venue's crockery but have to bring their own. As regards food itself, it seems that good practice is that either the organisation provides it or you bring your own. The 'plate supper' or 'bring and share' sociability is out of favour. But at least such meetups are happening for real, and not by Zoom. If that is what it takes to meet during the winter, so be it. I have still to find out what the local cinema requires. A meal at the pub and walk to the cinema nearby is a staple of winter social life for me.

But getting around and about as I have these last months, I have come to realise there are several ways we meet together. Sometimes, as above, it is as 'groups' with a Leader, sometimes in 'meetings', particularly to hear someone's great idea. Both of these suppose repeated attendance and regular faces. Or we might be in a 'crowd', just a nameless collection of folk who have come together in a haphazard sort of way. We have the 'Assembly' Rooms in Worthing, for performances and concerts of all genres. But that's sitting down and inside. On a summer's day but beginning to think about autumn, with heavy rain in the morning and windy afternoon, I wanted out.

In short, none of the above were quite right for celebrating, as now seems possible, if not the end of Covid, at least the end of restricted living. Wasn't there something more relaxed than groups? Something that was more informal than a group and with participants in the numbers that were disallowed in Covid restricted times. Something with some kind of point of contact or purpose so not by chance. I wanted a 'gathering'. You could have a group meet on Zoom, or stumble upon a website by chance, but not a 'gathering'.

So where could I go for a gathering? *Fun Day* at High Salvington Windmill offered a good answer. I could savour the taste of freedom now we are finished with all social distancing constraints, though one or two are wearing masks, as I have continued to do so largely on buses, and sometimes in shops. No requirement to book and there would certainly be more than 30 people around: lockdown's maximum number for outdoor happenings. Also 'gathering' sounds more appropriate for those enjoying a gentle friendly family Sunday afternoon at the Mill not by top-down summons, but by individual choice and decision.

There was no holding back on the happiness and simple excitement of the afternoon, the laughing, talking, gleeful shouting. It brought out the 'Inner Child' in me. What name would I give that really big teddy bear? Could I hook a plastic yellow duck? What fun to throw a floppy beanbag down the hole! What's that to 'splat the rat? I'm sure no rats are hurt in the playing of this game!

I should, would, leave it all to the real children, and 'play grown-ups'. Maybe have a flutter on the raffle, or join the buzz of booklovers around that busy stall. Or I could take it easy and sit with tea and cake and enjoy the lightfoot skills and intricate armplay of colourful and musical morris dancing.

Thus, I continued to be one but together with others, as I had not been able to these last 18 months. I had gone to the shops in a functional way. I had walked, marched, along the seafront, at the same time as other people. I had been in the same place as others in shopping precincts. I had met others in organised groups. This was just that different, walking as one but together with others, slowing down, speeding up, stopping, turning, creating flow and counter-flow, each contributing to the pleasure of all in the afternoon.

And there was a point of interest in the gathering. The Mill itself was central to the event. High Salvington Windmill[74] has a long history: as a working mill, then of becoming a tourist attraction with tearooms. More recently, it has been restored to full working and grinding capacity by volunteers, and so to heritage status. Its story is told in the recently published book 'High Salvington: Saving Worthing's last Windmill'.[75]

After its Covid-19 sleep, it was a great relief and delight to see the Mill returned to life, and to meet and greet fellow volunteers. Yet if I am recording that the Mill is back in business, so ends my self-appointed task of recording life in lockdown.

Or rather, so ends my record of how we, the people of Worthing (and beyond) have all contributed, have all kept each other going in lockdown, just by doing the job, adapting it, keeping at it, in shops, on transport, in

---

74   High Salvington Windmill, https://highsalvingtonwindmill. co.uk/

75   P. Casebow, 'High Salvington: Saving Worthing's last Windmill'. Mills Archive Trust. ISSN 2051-6924. 2021

our medical and personal care services, in town services, in hospitality, leisure and recreation facilities, the while offering individual help and encumbered by Covid security.

I walked across the grass to the teabar for a cup of tea and piece of cake and paid by contactless. What's new? It was the first time I had seen the contactless kit at the Mill, so I was full of respect for the aplomb whereby the which, what, where of the gadgetry was dib-dob-dabbed. 'Back in business', does not mean back to business where we were. It means back in business where we are. This collection of blogs has been an attempt to record how we came to be where we are, from where we were.

Long live the Mill!

Postscript

Two Summaries about life in lockdown follow, one formal, an outline of 'lockdown laws', the other my own, an informal collection of lockdown phrases.

PS 1. Outline of 'Lockdown laws'

from 23 March 2020 to 19 July 2021 (selected as seems relevant to my situation only)

Source: Coronavirus: A History of 'Lockdown laws' in England by Jennifer Brown, Esme Kirk-Wade (House of Commons Library), 22 December 2021,[76] and related sources.

England in Lockdown
from 23 March 2020

People must stay home, and preferably work from home. They should leave only if essential such as for shopping, or medical care. People may exercise, but one household alone and once a day only. Social distancing (two metres apart) has to be maintained.

Non-essential high street businesses must close, including personal care.

Hospitality venues must close, also other premises such as libraries, outdoor gyms and places of worship.

---

76   Contains Parliamentary information licensed under the Open Parliament Licence v3.0.

Relaxation
from 13 May 2020

People may leave home for unlimited exercise and recreation. They can meet one person from another household in open air spaces.

from 1 June 2020

Six people can meet in a group outside, which includes private gardens.

from 15 June 2020

Wearing a face covering on public transport becomes mandatory, unless exempt.

from 4 July 2020

Two households can meet indoors. No more than 30 people can gather outdoors.

Hospitality and personal care may re-open. Staycations are permitted.

from 27 July 2020

Wearing a face covering in shops and supermarkets becomes mandatory, unless exempt.

from 8 August 2020

Wearing a face covering becomes mandatory in indoor settings, such as museums and cinemas, unless exempt.

Return of Restrictions
from 14 September 2020

No more than six people can meet together – both indoors and out.

Hospitality venues must operate a table service only and close from 10pm to 6am.

The Three Tier System of Restrictions
from 14 October – 4 November 2020
Most of the country including Worthing is placed in Tier 1 (medium), with restrictions continuing unchanged.

Lockdown 2
from 5 November – 2 December 2020
National Restrictions are introduced. People can leave home only for specific reasons and can meet one person not of their household or support bubble outdoors, only.

Non-essential high street businesses, including personal care and hospitality must close but takeaways and deliveries are allowed.

Four Tier System
from 2 December 2020
Most of the country is placed in Tier 2 or 3. Worthing is placed in Tier 2 (high alert).

Different households can meet, in groups up to 6, outdoors only.

Pubs and restaurants can open to serve alcohol only with substantial meals, only by table service, and must close at 11pm.

from 20 December 2020
Worthing is moved to Tier 3, (very high alert).

Only those of the same household can meet in the garden or indoors. Outdoors up to 6 people can meet.

Hospitality venues must close but takeaways are allowed.

from 26 December 2020
Worthing is moved into Tier 4, essentially local lockdown.

People may not leave home without a 'reasonable excuse' but can meet one other person only in public outdoor spaces.

Non-essential retail must close, but click and collect is allowed.

Hospitality can operate only via takeaway or delivery.

Lockdown 3.
from 6 January 2021
National Restrictions introduced.

People should stay home but can meet one other not of their household or support bubble, for exercise outdoors. They cannot meet for organized recreation. Non-essential high street business must close including personal care.

The Road Map
22 February 2021
The Prime Minister makes a statement to the House of Commons setting out a 4-step roadmap out of lockdown, with effect from 8 March 2021.

not before 8 March 2021
People can meet one person from another household for recreation but must maintain social distancing.

not before 29 March 2021
Up to six people can meet, from two households and outdoors only but including in private gardens.

Outdoor sports facilities can re-open and organised outdoor sport.

not before 12 April 2021
No more than 6 people can meet and outdoors only
Non-essential retail, personal care services, indoor leisure facilities, and public libraries can reopen.
Restaurants and pubs can open for outdoor service.

not before 17 May 2021
Up to six people can meet indoors, or two households only. Hospitality can re-open indoors. Indoor group sports and exercise can re-open.
Outdoor gatherings of up to 30 can meet. The majority of the indoor and outdoor economy can reopen.

not before 21 June 2021
All legal restrictions to be lifted. However, with Covid numbers high, this was delayed until 19 July 2021.

not before 19 July 2021 (after the June date was postponed)
After the postponement from 21 June, all legal limits on social contact are lifted.
All remaining businesses can reopen.

PS 2. A Covid Vocabulary

Covid-19 : Covid : Lockdown (1, 2 & 3)
New normal : Tier System (1–3 and 1–4)

Stay at home : Protect the NHS : Save lives
Stay alert : Stay local

Clinically vulnerable : Shielding : Support bubble
Priority delivery : Priority hour

NHS rainbow : Nightingale Hospital : PPE
Thursday Clapping : Long Covid

Key worker : Frontline worker : Working from home

Home schooling : Zoom : Online classes

Social distance : Stay two metres apart : One-metre plus
Keep your distance : Stand back : Rule of six applies

Hands : face : space : Hand sanitiser : Anti-bac
Elbow bump : Wash your hands for 20 sec.
Wash your hands more often

(Non)-essential retail : Closed for the duration
Only (2) in shop at a time : One in one out policy

Queue this way : Keep hands and handles clean
Covid-secure : Stand behind the screen
One way : Exit this way

Cashless venue : Contactless preferred
E-tickets only : Collect here

Test & Trace : Covid-19 app : Pinged : Rapid flow test
PCR : Tested positive : Self-isolating

Face coverings must be worn : Mandatory
Face shields : Medically exempt : Breathable
Keep open for ventilation

Table service only : Eat out to Help out
Not yet sanitised

Vaccine : Jab : Jabbed : Antivax
Booster : Covid pass

Variant of Concern : Kent (renamed Alpha) variant
Indian (renamed Delta) variant

Ask reception for more tea/coffee : Travel corridors
Red/green/amber lists : Quarantine

Downing Street Briefing : Guided by the Science
The R-number : Roadmap
Government expects and recommends
Follow Government guidelines : Personal responsibility

Lockdown-Weary : Covid-Weary

This book is printed on paper from sustainable sources managed under the Forest Stewardship Council (FSC) scheme.

It has been printed in the UK to reduce transportation miles and their impact upon the environment.

For every new title that Matador publishes, we plant a tree to offset CO_2, partnering with the More Trees scheme.

For more about how Matador offsets its environmental impact, see www.troubador.co.uk/about/